JAMMU AND KASHMIR IN INDIA
THE SAGA OF DEVELOPMENT

Sheikh Khalid Jehangir

Published by
Renu Kaul Verma
Vitasta Publishing Pvt Ltd
4348/4C, Ansari Road, Daryaganj
New Delhi - 110 002
info@vitastapublishing.com

ISBN: 978-81-19670-13-0
© International Centre for Peace Studies
First Edition 2024
MRP ₹495

All Rights Reserved.
No part of this publication may be reproduced, stored in a retrieval system, or transmitted in any form, or by any means–electronic, mechanical, photocopying, recording or otherwise–without the prior permission of the publisher.
The views and opinions expressed in this book are the author's own. The publisher is in no way responsible for the same. While every effort has been made to verify the accuracy of the information presented, the publisher disclaims any responsibility for errors or omissions.

Typeset and Cover Design by Somesh Kumar Mishra
Printed by Chaman Enterprises, New Delhi

Union Territories Of Jammu & Kashmir And Ladakh

Source: https://static.pib.gov.in/WriteReadData/userfiles/Map%20of%20UTs.pdf
https://www.pib.gov.in/PressReleseDetailm.aspx?PRID=1590112

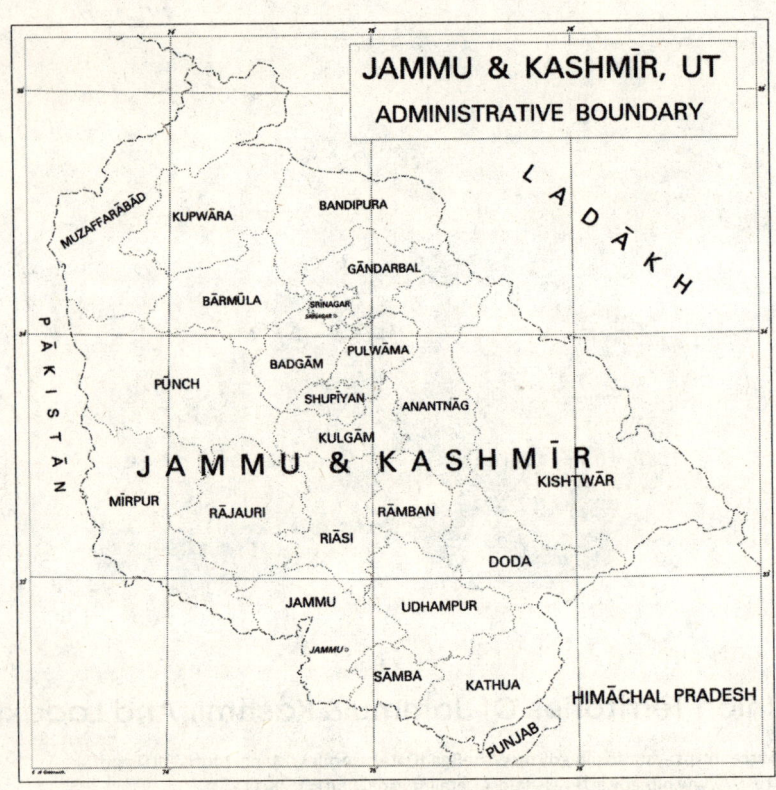

Jammu & Kashmir, UT Administrative Boundary
Source: https://static.pib.gov.in/WriteReadData/userfiles/UT%20of%20J&K.pdf

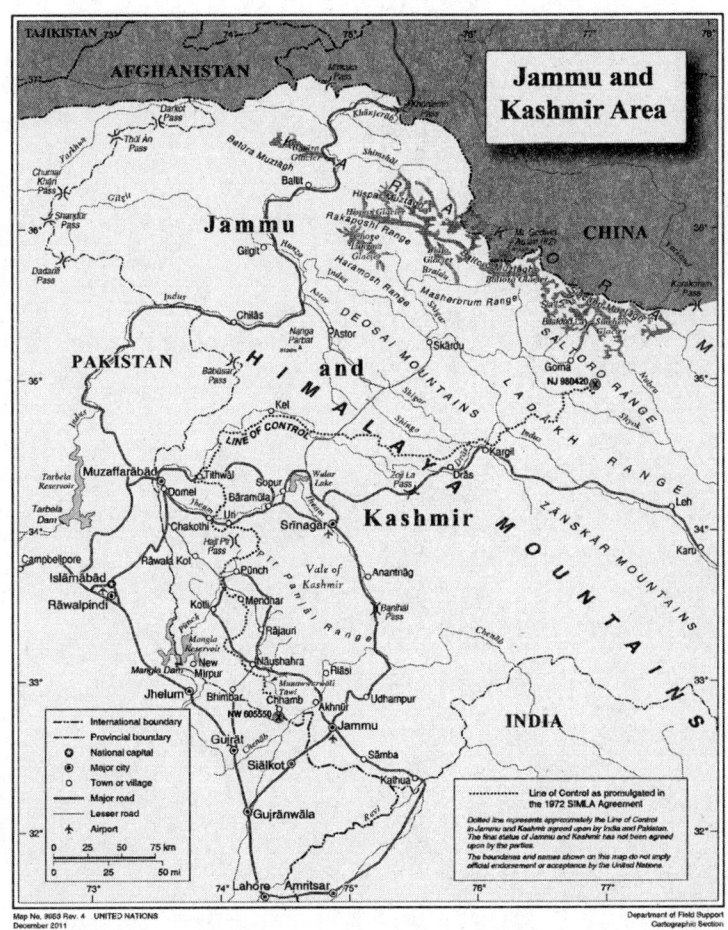

UN Map of Jammu and Kashmir Area Showing the Line of Control

Source: https://www.un.org/geospatial/file/2006/download?token=H9q3B2Zx

Contents

Abbreviations	*ix*
List of Tables	*xiii*
List of Figures	*xv*
Introduction	*xvii*

Chapter I — 1
The State and People of Kashmir
Tracing the Economic History

Chapter II — 33
J&K in India (1947-1989)
Beginning of Development

Chapter III — 50
Sponsored Militancy (1989-1998)
The Forced Backslide

Chapter IV — 71
Revival of Democratic Governance (1998-2019)
Developmental Lag

Chapter V — 109
Unleashing the Growth Impetus
J&K Since the Repeal of Article 370

Conclusion	*163*
Notes	*171*
Select Bibliography	*189*

Abbreviations

AIIMS	All India Institute for Medical Sciences
BCCI	Board of Cricket Control India
BADP	Border Area Development Programme
BDCs	Block Development Councils
BJP	Bharatiya Janata Party
CAG	Comptroller and Auditor General of India
CAGR	Cumulative Aggregate Growth Rate
CBI	Central Bureau of Investigation
CIS	Central Interest Subvention
CFL	Cease Fire Line
CGA	Comptroller General of Accounts
CLU	Change of Land Use
COP	Cost of Production
DDCs	District Development Councils
ED	Enforcement Directorate
FDI	Foreign Direct Investment
FIR	First Information Report
GDP	Gross Domestic Product
GSDP	Gross State Domestic Product

GSTLI	Goods & Services Tax Linked Incentive
GSVA	Gross State Value Added
HP	Himachal Pradesh
IAY	Indira Awas Yojna
INC	Indian National Congress
INR	Indian Rupee
J&K	Jammu and Kashmir
JKCA	Jammu and Kashmir Cricket Association
JKFDC	Jammu & Kashmir Film Development Council
LoC	Line of Control
MGNREGA	Mahatma Gandhi National Rural Employment Guarantee Act
MHA	Ministry of Home Affairs
MICE	Meetings, Incentives, Conferences & Exhibition
MPLADS	Members of Parliament Local Area Development Scheme
NC	National Conference
NCRB	National Crime Records Bureau
NDA	National Democratic Alliance
NIA	National Investigating Agency
NRHM	National Rural Health Mission
NSDP	Net State Domestic Product
OSD	Office on Special Duty
PDP	People's Democratic Party
PMLA	Prevention of Money Laundering Act
PMGSY	Pradhan Mantri Gram Sadak Yojana
PoJK	Pakistan Occupied Jammu and Kashmir
RERA	Real Estate (Regulation & Development) Act
SAC	State Accountability Commission
SEZ	Special Economc Zone
SIAs	State Implementing Agencies

SIT	Special Investigation Team
SRE	Security Related Expenditure
UT	Union Territory
WCIS	Working Capital Interest Subvention

List of Tables

Table 2.1 Key developments and legislation   36

Table 2.2 J&K's revenue receipts over the years   45

Table 3.1 Annual budget allocations during 1990-97   56

Table 3.2 J&K's revenue receipts during the
           1988-98 period   58

Table 3.3 Trend of J&K's revenue account   60

Table 3.4 Loans and advances from the
           Central Government   64

Table 3.5 Jammu & Kashmir NSDP at current rates vs
           neighbouring states (crores)   66

Table 3.6 Per Capita NSDP at current prices (Rs)   68

Table 4.1 Comparison of GSDP of J&K with GSDP of
           neighbouring states (crores)   74

Table 4.2 Comparison of per capita income (per capita
           NSDP at current prices) of J&K with those
           of neighbouring states   74

Table 4.3 Total Central Government assistance to J&K (1998-2019)	77
Table 4.4 Funds transferred directly to State Implementing Agencies during 2008-09 (crores)	81
Table 4.5 Funds transferred directly to State Implementing Agencies during 2009-10 (crores)	83
Table 4.6 J&K self-revenue receipts	86
Table 4.7 Grant-in-aid provided by the state to autonomous bodies/authorities	95
Table 5.1 Number of terrorism incidents (2018-2021)	112
Table 5.2 GSDP of J&K (crores)	120
Table 5.3 Comparison of GSDP (at constant prices) of J&K with neighbouring states	122
Table 5.4 Comparison of per capita income (at current prices) of J&K with neighbouring states	124
Table 5.5 Number of tourist arrivals in J&K	149

List of Figures

Figure 2.1 Trend of central assistance to J&K — 46

Figure 2.2 Trend of central assistance to J&K — 47

Figure 3.1 Annual revenue and capital allocations — 57

Figure 3.2 Grants-in-aid in J&K's revenue receipts — 59

Figure 3.3 Revenue surplus (crores) — 61

Figure 3.4 Central assistance against J&K's revenue receipts — 61

Figure 3.5 J&K's own revenue vs central assistance (1988-98) — 62

Figure 3.6 Central assistance vs J&K's own resources as percentage of J&K's total revenue receipts — 63

Figure 3.7 Trend of J&K's NSDP at current prices during 1990-99 period — 65

Figure 3.8 NSDP of J&K vs HP, Punjab & Haryana at current prices (crores) — 66

Figure 3.9 J&K's per capita NSDP at current prices against neighbouring states — 67

Figure 4.1	Trend of central grant-in-aid assistance to J & K (1998-2019)	78
Figure 4.2	Annual trend of J&K's share in central tax collection (1998-2019)	78
Figure 4.3	Trend of Central Government assistance to J&K (1998-2019)	80
Figure 4.4	Percentage change in Central Government assistance to J&K (1998-2019)	81
Figure 4.5	Contribution of J&K's self-generated resources to total revenue receipts (1998-2019)	85
Figure 4.6	Trend of J & K's self-generated resources revenue receipts (1998-2019)	87
Figure 4.7	Composition of J & K's revenue receipts	93
Figure 5.1	Trend of J&K's GSDP growth rate	121
Figure 5.2	Comparison of J&K's CAGR of GSDP (at constant price) with neighbouring states	122
Figure 5.3	J&K's revenue receipts (2020-21)	129

Introduction

There has been a great deal of negative propaganda in Kashmir over the years about the stepmotherly attitude shown by New Delhi towards Kashmir and Kashmiris. It is part of the consistent cross-border campaign to show India in a bad light among the people of Kashmir and to tarnish India's image at home and abroad. This has been so because of various reasons. An atmosphere of distrust and pessimism has been created in Kashmir, which has helped spoilers to spawn damaging accounts of India, and a conducive environment has been created at the same time at the international level to propel such narratives.

During the Cold War period, when Pakistan cosied up to the West, there was a visible tilt in the perception of the liberal world towards the Pakistani position on Kashmir. It was regarded as natural that a Muslim-majority region would accede to Pakistan. What the policymakers and analysts in the liberal world forgot was that India did not accept partition along religious lines, and the decision was taken with a very heavy heart to avert violence and bloodshed in undivided India. What they forgot further was that India developed itself as a secular liberal democratic state, and the people of Jammu and Kashmir (J&K), after their horrifying experience with the tribal *lashkars* from Pakistan in October

1947, had helped Indian soldiers in repulsing the invaders. Later, they participated enthusiastically in the first constituent assembly elections in 1951 following which in 1954, the elected assembly ratified the state's accession to India. The constitution of the state came into force in January 1957 and endorsed the accession.

While Pakistan insisted on communal logic, India went ahead with its experience of secular democracy, where state identity was not to be defined in terms of one religion or another. Rather than accepting such a liberal ideal, there was sympathy amongst the liberal democratic countries of the world (who identified themselves as the 'free world') towards the Pakistani logic that a Muslim-majority Kashmir ought to have merged with Pakistan, which claimed to be an Islamic State, a state where both religious and ethnic minorities have been treated with disdain.

Pakistan went ahead with the propagation of its communal logic in Kashmir as well, gradually infecting the local mindset with its acerbic anti-India propaganda. In the process, the seeds of secessionism were sown in the minds of the Kashmiri people, who had valiantly repulsed the tribal lashkars sent in by Pakistan to forcibly secure Kashmir's accession to Pakistan. In the aftermath of the tribal invasion, almost one-third of the territory of Jammu and Kashmir remained under Pakistani occupation. India's bid to get it back through United Nations (UN)-led international mediation and pressure came to nought because the most powerful of the permanent members of the UN Security Council bought the Pakistani argument that India was sidestepping the rationale of partition on communal lines and usurping the rightful claim of Pakistan to Kashmir.

While the situation gradually started taking a turn for the better after the end of the Cold War, the inertia of those years has continued to colour the visions of powerful nations about Kashmir.

All this has, inevitably, had ramifications inside Kashmir. There was a continuous effort to drum up anti-India sentiments and incite innocent people to violence. Pakistan even resorted to the use of war in 1965 as a catalyst for insurgency in Kashmir, believing that there would be a spontaneous outpouring of sympathy for Pakistan amongst the Kashmiris in 1965 and the armed insurrection would assume such a shape that India would be forced to surrender Kashmir to Pakistan. In 1971, Pakistan resorted to a similar tactic and failed, losing control of territories north of Turtuk to India.

In 1999, it launched the Kargil war and had to withdraw, resulting in heavy casualties on its side, with its soldiers dying unsung and their bodies lying unclaimed. Such repeated failures of the Pakistani strategy of engaging India in direct or indirect war have not stopped it from using terrorism as a strategy against India. Added to this is the information warfare it has unleashed to bring down India's reputation in the comity of nations.

A section of Kashmiris has repeatedly fallen prey to the Pakistani disinformation campaign over the years. Pakistan's military establishment has exploited every type of media, including frontline conventional and new age (social) media, to that end. The often repeated propaganda trope of the Pakistani establishment and their local partners in Kashmir has revolved around the narrative of victimisation at the hands of India, often peddling false statistics and half-baked facts to claim that the poor socio-economic conditions prevailing in Kashmir is a result of the apathy shown by the government in New Delhi. Their oft-repeated narrative, is predicated on the baseless accusation that India's policy has been to deal with the Kashmiris through a communal lens, as a majority of the population is Muslim and hence this is the basis for denying the people of J&K the right to manage their affairs on their own.

Unfortunately, many a time, the local political actors—who have been part of the electoral politics in J&K—have also, over the years, fanned negative emotions about India. They have accused New Delhi of not extending liberal financial packages to the region and creating a situation in which the state is perpetually dependent on the Central Government.

In this context, the findings presented in this book suggest that the reality in J&K is vastly different. The data-laden exhaustive analysis in Chapters II–IV clearly disproves any claim whatsoever that the Indian government has pursued a discriminatory policy to deliberately 'underdevelop' Kashmir over the years. On the contrary, Kashmir has always received disproportionate attention in the sense that the per capita investment by India in Kashmir has been way above its investments in other important states bordering J&K. The central grants to Kashmir are also far in excess of the revenue the state has collected year after year.

Jammu and Kashmir was given special status, so that the state could handle all local governance functions in an autonomous way, within the broader ambit of the Constitution of India. However, this was misused by successive local political leaderships to create a culture of nepotism and corruption, often exploiting the statutory protection of Article 370 to escape the oversight of the national accountability mechanism of the country.

It also emerges from the findings that the state had witnessed rapid developmental activity every time there was Central Government rule. However, even those years were mostly wasted in terms of the generation of human capital in the state. This was because a culture of anarchy and violence was carefully constructed by vested interest groups in the state, with aid from outside. This overpowered the imagination of the people, mostly the youth, and they were consequently influenced by the resultant politics of hatred and ignominy.

The state and its people have suffered heavily for allowing themselves to be used as cannon fodder by forces outside Kashmir across the border and being unable to see through their pretension of sincerity and devotion to the so-called 'cause' of Kashmir.

The data collected in the book also wakes us up to another important reality that has hardly ever been discussed in Kashmir. The first chapter in the book dwells on the economic history of the Kashmir region over centuries, when the Kashmiris were seen to be operating under the yoke of oppression even if the rulers changed from the indigenous ones to the Mughals, the Pathans and finally, the Dogras. The data shows how the taxation system imposed on the people was one of the most repressive and alienating, and the rights and dignity of the individual were sacrificed at the altar of the state that was ruled with an iron hand by kings and monarchs of bygone eras. In contrast, the experience of democracy and liberty immediately after Kashmir acceded to the Indian Union was certainly like a breath of fresh air for a people long subjugated to tyrannical rule. The people experienced freedom and human rights under the Indian Constitution, and the revenue system that was introduced was certainly far more progressive than any other system that was in vogue in the past.

The transformative impact of the democratic and developmental administration in Kashmir after it joined the Union of India has not been valued by the people of Kashmir, because they have not reflected on it deeply and have not also compared it with the experience of the people living under illegal occupation in Pakistan Occupied Jammu and Kashmir (PoJK). The author of this book had dwelt on this in his last book, *The Two Kashmirs*, published in October 2022, wherein data was presented from both sides of Kashmir. This clearly showed how lopsided the economic situation was in PoJK compared to

Kashmir in India. The lack of political freedom and economic alienation in PoJK came out starkly in the findings.

The present book may be considered an extension of or a sequel to that book. It seeks to bring out data on the resources allocated and to the developmental initiatives undertaken by the Central Government over the years and to show that the abrogation of Article 370 by the Indian Parliament on 5 August 2019 has not impeded the process of allocation of developmental funds to the state. In fact, there has been greater allocation of funds and a clear spurt in developmental activities in J&K, which is visible in terms of superior infrastructure and investments in roads, power, health, education, tourism, agriculture, skill development, and other sectors.

Various projects languishing in the state for over 10 to 20 years were completed with investments of more than Rs 2,000 crores. A total of 17,601 km of road was constructed under the Pradhan Mantri Gram Sadak Yojna till March 2022, which has connected 2,074 destinations. On 20 February 2024, Prime Minister Narendra Modi inaugurated the Banihal-Sangaldan Railway Line and flagged off the first electric train in the Kashmir Valley from Baramulla station. This line, constructed with an expenditure of Rs 15,863 crores, is set to revolutionise transportation in Kashmir.

In the educational sphere too, the state has taken giant strides. The state has witnessed the establishment of two new All India Institute for Medical Sciences (AIIMS), seven new medical colleges, two State cancer institutes and 15 nursing colleges with a capacity of 854 seats. J&K has also seen the operationalisation of the Indian Institute of Technology (IIT) Jammu and the Indian Institute of Management (IIM) Jammu. The number of government degree/engineering colleges has gone up from 96 to 147.

Between 2020 and 2022, power projects with a combined

capacity of about 3,000 MW were revived. Kashmiri saffron has been given a GI (geographical indication) tag, and the high-density plantation scheme has been extended from apple to mango, litchi, walnut and cherry. The Jal Jeevan Mission has been taken up with due seriousness by the local administration. In fact, Srinagar and Ganderbal can now claim to have 100 per cent allocation of water to all households (*Har Ghar Jal*). Tap water connections in the rest of the districts have increased from 5.75 lakh households (31 per cent) to 10.55 lakh households (57 per cent). Irrigation projects like the main Ravi canal, Tral lift-irrigation and flood management-cum-irrigation on the Jhelum have been completed. The number of youths employed during the last three years is around 30,000 and there are self-employment schemes too to provide income for about 5 lakh people.

Cumulatively, J&K has received Rs 58,477 crores in various sectors to fund about 53 major projects so far. It has also received applications for industrial investment of more than Rs 54,000 crores, out of which projects worth more than Rs 36,000 crores have been allotted land to build their infrastructure at the earliest. The volume and pace of development introduced in J&K in the last four years have been so encouraging that the people of the region now realise that the three decades lost to terrorism and insurgency could have set in motion a revolutionary growth dynamic to the envy of the rest of the Indian states.

This book makes a sincere attempt to provide evidence for the assertions being made here in the introduction. The chapters are arranged chronologically with utmost emphasis given to the years of insurgency and the present phase to emphasise the point that even when the pathology of hatred against India was at its height, New Delhi went ahead with its developmental allocations for the state. The approach of the Indian state towards Kashmir was conditioned by the thinking that the local elite would create an environment of trust, understanding and harmony that would reverse the senseless violence and lay the foundations of a better tomorrow. However, as has been made clear in this book, the local leadership did not show any sign of maturity and did everything possible, whether wittingly or unwittingly, to normalise terrorism and violence and thereby quietly encouraged Kashmiris to take up arms against the state.

A situation emerged where empathy for terror was mixed with apathy towards the state system, creating a volatile political atmosphere and spirit of insanity that militated against the unity and integrity of the state. With the special status gone after August 2019, the forces of instability suffered a big jolt, and the vested interest groups who had softened the approach of the state towards militancy were disabled, unleashing a fresh impulse for change in Jammu and Kashmir. It has, so far, paid us well, and if it continues, it will augur a new era of peace and progress for the state and its people.

In putting this book together, I have taken the help of a number of people who should be mentioned here to duly record my obligations. This book would not have been possible, but for the untiring efforts put in by Dr Waseem Malla and Dr Syed Eesar Mehdi, both research fellows at the International Centre for Peace Studies (ICPS). They mined data for the volume and helped me with the analysis of the data as well. It was a great learning experience for me while I was finalising all the chapters of the book. I hope the readers will appreciate the efforts that we have put together and the book will provoke wider discussion on the theme.

Sheikh Khalid Jehangir

New Delhi
31 March 2024

Chapter I

The State and People of Kashmir
Tracing the Economic History

Background

THE PRINCELY state of Jammu and Kashmir (J&K) emerged as a prominent entity in British India in 1846. This region comprised distinct regions: the Kashmir Valley, Jammu, and Ladakh.[1] These areas exhibited diverse landscapes and populations. The Kashmir valley had a predominantly Muslim population, Jammu was mostly Hindu and Ladakh had a mix of Buddhists and Muslims. Prior to this, Jammu and Kashmir were under the rule of the Afghans (1753-1819) and later, the Sikhs (1819-46). These rulers appointed governors—fourteen during Afghan rule and twelve during Sikh rule.

In 1819, Gulab Singh, a significant member of a Dogra Rajput family working under the Sikhs, captured Kashmir. As a reward, he was given control of Jammu in 1820 and was permitted by Maharaja Ranjit Singh, the illustrious Sikh ruler, to collect taxes there. Gulab Singh assumed the title of 'Raja of Jammu' in 1822.[2] Under Sikh rule, Gulab Singh and his brothers, Dhyan Singh and Suchet Singh, accumulated land and wealth in both the flatlands and the hilly regions in Punjab bordering Jammu and Kashmir.[3] In a short span of time, they gained control over 85 *jagirs* bordering the Kashmir Valley. In 1834, Zorawar Singh, a Wazir of Gulab Singh, successfully led a campaign to conquer Ladakh, which was subsequently integrated with Jammu. Similarly, between 1839 and 1840, Zorawar brought Baltistan under the control of the Raja of Jammu. This raised the status of the Dogras under Sikh rule. However, after the death of Ranjit Singh and the decline of the Sikh empire, Gulab Singh leaned towards the British. Following the defeat of the Sikhs in the First Anglo-Sikh War in 1846 and their inability to meet British demands, they were compelled to cede territories, including Kashmir and Hazara (currently in Khyber Pakhtunkhwa, Pakistan), situated between the Beas and Indus rivers.[4] The British, however, could not occupy these northern areas directly for themselves due to lack of resources, as they had only recently captured parts of Punjab. Their existing dominion in 1846 concluded at the Sutlej River, significantly distant from the Valley of Kashmir. The British East India Company also sought to recognise Gulab Singh for his support during its Punjab campaigns. Consequently, through the Treaty of Amritsar, the Company sold Jammu, Kashmir and Ladakh to Gulab Singh for 75 lakh Nanakshahi Rupees, equivalent to £750,000. This gesture acknowledged his allegiance to the British Crown and definitively demarcated the boundaries of the princely state of Jammu and Kashmir.[5]

The Treaties

After the fall of the Sikh empire in 1846, a pivotal shift took place in the trajectory of regional geopolitics, as the East India Company consummated two consequential treaties. The first of these, known as the Treaty of Lahore, was solemnised in Lahore on 9 March 1846, engendering an accord between the British authorities and the Sikhs. This entente facilitated the recognition of Dalip Singh as the reigning Maharaja, on the Lahore throne, albeit under the protective auspices of British suzerainty. The second accord, named the Treaty of Amritsar, was executed on 16 March 1846, signifying a compact between the British East India Company and Gulab Singh, thereby engendering the formal establishment of the princely dominion of Jammu and Kashmir. This nascent political entity encompassed an expanse that included Jammu, Kashmir, Ladakh, Hunza, Nagar, Gilgit and Baltistan. It merits attention here that the contracting parties to this arrangement were confined to the British East India Company and Gulab Singh.

The Treaty of Amritsar, while conventionally viewed as an expression of gratitude to Gulab Singh for his ostensible neutrality during the tumultuous phase of Anglo-Sikh hostilities, involved financial considerations. Gulab Singh was required to pay for the ceded territories accorded to him by the British.[6] Pertinently, Article VIII of the Treaty concretised the sovereignty of Gulab Singh in a contingent manner, predicated upon his adherence to an assortment of 'Articles of Engagement' between the East India Company and Lahore's Sikh incumbents on 11 March 1846. This stipulatory edifice committed the British to safeguard the lawful entitlements of the *jagirdars* (landholders) appointed by the Sikh administration in the relinquished territorial domains, thereby warranting the perpetuity of their possession throughout their lifespans.[7]

By corollary, the newly vested Dogra authority was thereby duty-bound to accept these *jagirs* as grants extended to the Sikh royal progeny, state functionaries, and individuals of social eminence, thereby concomitantly circumscribing the modalities of revenue accrual. The Treaty of Amritsar further engendered the construct of a 'subsidiary alliance' between the Dogras and the British, a configuration enunciated the historical literature.[8] Notably, it was within this schema that the Dogra dynasts acknowledged the preeminent authority of British paramountcy and thereby acquiesced to satisfying tributary obligations.[9] An integral clause of the Treaty was to define and delineate the frontiers with precision, which helped demarcate the territorial confines of the princely state, and it precluded any alteration 'without the concurrence of the British government'[10] Evidently, the institutional representation of the Maharaja's prerogatives, encompassing attributes of 'rights and privileges,' and notably 'sovereignty and power,' carried a veneer of symbolism that aligned them with analogous manifestations in contemporaneous princely states. In this regard, the precedent of Jammu and Kashmir substantiates an overarching pattern manifest in other princely domains, characterised by the predominance of the unbounded leverage of British hegemony, transcending the constraints imposed by treaty-based interventions.[11]

Following the signing of the Treaty, the British authority engaged in an iterative process of admonishing the Dogra polity concerning the necessity of instituting an efficient state administration. One of the pivotal thrusts of these exhortations entailed the imperative of extending the ambit of the administrative jurisdiction through the deployment of official personnel across the entire territorial extent of the state.[12] Navnita Chadha Behera, a discerning commentator, underscores that the nominal independence retained by the state of Jammu and Kashmir, despite its exclusion from British territorial dominion, was circumscribed by factors of a complex nature.[13] This observation is underscored by Chitralekha Zutshi, who points to the multi-layered dialectics between Kashmir and various tracts constituting the British Indian landscape. This mediating prism of the Dogra state delineated a discernible pattern of colonial influence that was moderated by the indigenous power structure. This proclivity towards intermediation is paradigmatically evidenced in kindred instances across princely dominions such as Hyderabad and Baroda, thereby substantiating the broader contour of such modalities.[14]

Thus, the trajectory of colonial policy evinced a convergence of resistance and transformation through the prism of the Dogra state. This dynamic was discernible across several domains, albeit with variances contingent upon the situational exigency peculiar to each entity. Moreover, an underlying theme of emulation of colonial administrative mechanisms by the Dogra polity is also underscored by the evolution of administrative postures over the temporal arc. The appointment of an 'Officer on Special Duty (OSD)' in 1852, a role ostensibly designated to oversee European visitors to the realm of Kashmir, marks an early instance of British institutional involvement in the administrative realm.[15] This tentative incursion gained momentum as the status of the designated Officer transitioned to that of a resident (or colonial advisor to the native ruler) in the year 1885.[16] A notable shift happened in 1889, wherein the Maharaja's prerogatives were divested, thereby culminating in the constitution of an administrative council responsible for the governance of the state. The authority wielded by the council, which included its presiding dignitary, was largely perfunctory, with real power residing in the hands of the British Resident, who oversaw the activities of the council, ultimately assuming the role of definitive arbiter as well as arbiter in matters of governance.[17] Through such manoeuvre, the British exerted an efficacious influence over state administration, encompassing critical domains such as the assessment and collection of land revenue.

Revenue Practices in Earlier Times

Preceding the advent of the Dogra rule, the sociopolitical landscape of Kashmir witnessed a succession of historical shifts, marked by diverse rulers and dynastic ebbs and flows, intertwined with the evolution of statecraft and the concomitant mechanisms of revenue generation. Evident across these epochs was the persistent patronage practice of conferring land grants upon select family lineages for ensuring their continued fealty, a practice enduring over centuries. The financial sustenance of rulers was buttressed by a multifaceted taxation structure for the levying of land revenue upon agrarian producers. It is noteworthy, however, that comprehensive archival documentation elucidating the quantum of land revenue collected in the early medieval period remains conspicuously absent.

The crystallisation of a codified schema of land taxes, denominated *nasaq*, seems to have been a phenomenon of the Mughal epoch in the annals of Kashmir.[18] Land revenue remained the main source of income for the state exchequer in Kashmir, as in other kingdoms. Mughals introduced the method of assessment known as *Nasaqi-ghalla-bakhsh* for the total amount of revenue obtainable from the entirety of the arable land. One of the fundamental variables of this method was to ascertain the average per-unit yield of land. Aiming to perpetuate economic equilibrium and administrative order, Emperor Akbar dispatched a five-member team in 1589. The team was entrusted with the formulation of a blueprint for land revenue assessment alongside the delineation of the nature and scope of collection.[19] This endeavour culminated in an exhaustive compendium meticulously charting the topography of the land, its hierarchical classification, productivity attributes, and apportionment mechanisms. As underscored by Hangloo, this recalibration executed by the appointed envoys effectively counteracted the malfeasance of venal functionaries, who had historically appropriated the entitlements of both the state and the agrarian populace.[20] The outcome of this exercise was a comprehensive administrative reconfiguration. It was punctuated by the introduction of designations such as *patwari* (or *patwaree*), *tahsildar, amil, fotedar, munsif, qanungo, chaudhri, dewan* and other concomitant roles.[21]

Central to the architecture of revenue generation were activities interwoven with the agrarian sector; endeavours of artisans within villages, including woodcarving, woollen weaving, basketry, papier-mâché craftsmanship and metalworking with silver and copper; and the craftsmanship of shawls, carpets and leather goods. Predominantly concentrated around Srinagar, these industries were subjected to levies alongside import and export duties on an array of commodities. These thereby constituted a major revenue reservoir for the ruling elite, accentuated by the significance of shawl and carpet exports. Notwithstanding these revenue streams, the lynchpin of fiscal inflow remained tethered to land taxes, embracing both tangible produce and monetary levies. This underscores the strategic imperative to foster a flourishing tapestry of agricultural endeavours, inclusive of the cultivation of staple grains and orchard fruits.

Dogra Rulers and Revenue Policies

Following the Mughal era, there was a marked continuity of practices in the revenue sector in the subsequent Afghan, Sikh and Dogra periods, albeit with nuanced alterations, with regard to land endowments and the established frameworks for revenue generation. Among these, the Dogra sovereigns, in particular, extended *jagirs* to influential and devoted lineages as well as religious foundations as an acknowledgment of loyal service to the state, and in some cases, in response to political exigencies.[22] The institution of *jagirdari* not only conferred social prestige but also vested its beneficiaries with authority, particularly concerning the collection of revenues for the state. This structure, however, introduced an array of levies and taxes imposed upon the agricultural populace, thereby increasing the scope for corrupt practices within the domain of revenue administration. Instances arose wherein *jagirdars* exceeded their prescribed territorial jurisdictions and levied disproportionate taxes upon the agrarian class.

An important edict, issued by Maharaja Gulab Singh on 6 September 1847, preserved the intricate apparatus governing the apportionment of land to cultivators. This entailed meticulous calculations involving the state's entitlement to the produce, the valuation of grains, and the fixation of exchange rates. This replication of the methodology used by the Sikh rulers underscored the conceptualisation of the land as the ruler's domain, referred to as *Khalisa* under Islamic rulers such as the Delhi Sultanate and the Mughal Empire, with a portion conferred as *jagirs* and the remainder annually allocated to cultivators in proportion to their strength.[23] Importantly, P N K Bamzai's exposition brings to the fore the paradigm of the Dogra era, wherein the cultivators lacked rights of ownership or occupancy over the land they tilled. Instances of hereditary occupants was a rarity.[24] Their tenure was contingent upon the allocation decided by the *kardar*, the state-appointed custodian of cultivation-related matters, who was vested with oversight authority across a cluster of villages.[25]

Cultivators shouldered the burden of an elaborate ensemble of levies representing the state's share and incremental taxes periodically imposed by the ruler. Under Maharaja Gulab Singh's stewardship, the state's claim to the *kharif* crop (spring harvest) amounted to half the produce along with four *traks* per *kharwa*r (approximately 80 kg). Correspondingly, the Rabi crop (autumn harvest) incurred fifty per cent state collection along with three *traks* per *kharwar*, accompanied by sundry ancillary taxes.[26] Supplementary obligations included *nazarana*, a quarterly imposition, and *tambol*, a tribute payable during matrimonial festivities within the royal family, for instance. Noteworthy in this context is Zutshi's elucidation of the stratified nature of land taxes, with varying rates applied to distinct social strata. For example, the Kashmiri Pandits, Sayyids and Pirzadas–comprising the societal elite–were accorded preferential tax treatment.

Critical analyses underscore that the quantum of revenue exacted from cultivators during the Dogra dominion was significantly high. The correspondence dated 21 August 1878 of F Henvey, the Officer on Special Duty (OSD) in Kashmir, substantiates that although the government was entitled to approximately fifty per cent of the gross produce–particularly in kind–in all cases, this equity principle was not consistently observed. The discrepancy was most pronounced in the case of rice, where the state requisitioned a quantum exceeding fifty per cent from the *zamindar*, thus causing an imbalance. Consequently, this discordant arrangement engendered instances where revenue officials appropriated the entire crop during periods of scarcity.

Further in the context of this comprehensive array of levies, M S Khan in his book, *The History of Jammu and Kashmir: 1885-1925* writes citing contemporary sources that the peasantry was crushed under the burden of heavy taxation. He mentions that for every 32 *traks* of kharif yield, a mandated payment of 21 *traks* and 11.75 seers (equivalent to nearly two *traks*) was prescribed in kind. Correspondingly, for the Rabi crop, the stipulated contribution encompassed

20 *traks* and 6.75 seers in kind. In addition to these, recurrent levies comprised the *russo-dart*–an impost based on each village domicile's assessment, with rates ranging from 4 to 20 annas. The fruit tax, representing 75 per cent of the annual yield, alongside taxes imposed on livestock–two to three sheep and goats annually–and a yearly levy on ponies, collectively underscored the financial burdens borne by the cultivators. Moreover, specialised taxes applied to products such as tweed, poultry, ghee, honey and firewood. Furthermore, a tax was applied on crops such as wheat, barley, *mussoor*, flax, *oorud*, *tel*, *moong* and cotton. T D Forsyth, the Officiating Secretary to the Punjab Government, noted in 1863 that tax collection in Kashmir was conducted through a blend of cash and kind.[27] In-kind levies pertained to crops such as *shali* (or *shalee*, meaning rice or paddy) and wheat, while pecuniary exactions applied to tobacco and minor agricultural produce. Additionally, an array of taxes spanned diverse domains including sericulture, the shawl industry, horticulture, saffron cultivation, opium husk production, matrimonial registrations, and an assortment of artisanal and domestic occupations. Notably, these multifarious levies and imposts were frequently introduced during ceremonial events, with the collections channelled through an intricate web of intermediaries comprising state officials and community representatives. It merits mention that the British authorities deemed this operational structure inefficient in terms of revenue collection.

The regulation of grain commerce through state-controlled granaries, wherein prices were prescribed by administrative authorities, reflects a practice observed not only in Kashmir but also in other princely states. However, a shift in the late nineteenth century saw a deregulation of grain markets in several princely states, prompting the British to advocate a similar transformation in the context of Kashmir. This proposition was grounded in the argument that state oversight of grain trade fostered a culture of administrative corruption, particularly evident during periods of scarcity.

The imperative for a judiciously formulated land revenue settlement system and the effective administration of revenue garnered attention from figures such as Col R P Nisbet, who, in his letter to the Secretary of Government of India in January 1890, underscored the significance of devising an appropriate methodology and scale for collecting land revenue, given that 'over three-fourths of the revenue of the Kashmir state was derived from land and the cultivating classes.' The envisaged idea of further augmentation of agricultural revenue was based on the exceptional fertility of Kashmir's soil. The then Settlement Officer and the Officer on Special Duty concurred on the resourcefulness of Kashmiri cultivators, who demonstrated adeptness in adopting advanced agricultural practices such as grafting and diversifying crop cultivation, concurrent with their artisanal engagements. During periods of agricultural abundance, the region exhibited surplus grain production, adequately addressing the dietary needs of its populace.

The grain, once collected by state authorities, was stored in communal granaries and subsequently allocated at predetermined rates to various stakeholders, including the military, government officials, and urban residents. Nonetheless, from 1877 to 1880, adverse climatic conditions and natural disasters led to a dearth of grain available for equitable distribution among urban and rural communities. Official records attributed to F Henvey, Officer on Special Duty disclosed, in a note written to Government of Punjab in August 1878, that there was a substantial decline in the population of Srinagar, plummeting from 127,400 to 88,000 during this period, presumably caused by the famines. The observations from a French shawl trader during this period mentioned by Henvey indicated a stark contraction in the weaver population of Srinagar, dropping from nearly 30,000 to a mere 4,000 following the famines. This sort of paucity of skilled labour would typically engender inability to meet the demand from major foreign buyer countries, thereby perpetuating poverty.

Consequently, the British posited that recurrent famines[28] could be mitigated through the institution of a more efficient revenue settlement system. As expounded by Zutshi, the prevailing system was construed by the British as disordered and tainted by fraudulent practices. They contended that the provision of grains to the urban populace at fixed rates, in-kind tax collection, and compromised revenue administration collectively contributed to disruptions in the agricultural sector and impediments to the effective realisation of tax revenue.

Maharaja's Taxation System

Robert Thorp (1838-1868), a British military officer, visited Kashmir in 1865 and was profoundly stirred by the exploitative practices perpetuated under the Dogra rule. This led him to write the book *Cashmere Misgovernment*. This book stands as a significant exposition of the intricate tax structure imposed by the Maharaja within the context of Kashmir. Thorp's narrative[29] underscored the comprehensive appropriation of nearly all agricultural produce by the government and the multifaceted cadre of functionaries that was instrumental in its extraction, remunerated through allocations sourced from the *zamindars*. The subsequent enumeration delineated distinctive actors critical to the assemblage and allocation of agricultural output, while also encompassing broader administrative functions beyond the city of Srinagar. This administrative ambit was governed by the authority of the Governor of Kashmir and the Chief Magistrate. The principal among these officers were:

1. **Tehsildar:** Overseeing a jurisdiction of two to five *purgunnahs*, the *tehsildar* exercised supervisory authority over *kardars'* financial records within their designated district. Their prerogatives extended to the imposition of penalties, including imprisonment of up to a fortnight and fines not exceeding ten rupees. Additionally, the *tehsildar* arbitrated disputes, complaints, and infractions occurring within their tehsil. The *tehsildar's* command was upheld by a contingent of 200 to 400 *sepoys*, and their direct accountability was solely to the Diwan or the Governor of Kashmir, who resided within the city.

2. **Thanadar:** Occupying the foremost position within each *purgunnah*, the *thanadar* wielded lesser punitive authority, presiding over approximately 40 to 50 *sepoys*. Their remit encompassed conducting comprehensive inspections throughout their purgunnah and furnishing reports pertaining to agricultural produce and broader matters to their *tehsildar*.

3. **Kardar:** Holding a pivotal role among officials directly engaged in the aggregation of agricultural yield, the *kardar* assumed oversight of specified villages. Their remit encompassed meticulous documentation of crops within each village, coupled with personal supervision during harvest periods, thus ensuring equitable distribution. Besides, the *kardars* submitted reports to their respective *thanadars*, thus facilitating the dispatch of the government's share of the harvest to predetermined destinations as per directives. On occasion, the government accepted monetary compensation in lieu of specific grain categories from the *kardars*. This arrangement, however, frequently bore no consequence for the *zamindars*, as the *kardars* continued to exact the complete harvest from them, deriving personal benefit by selling the equivalent quantities

earmarked by the government. The discernible preference for this mode of transaction signified heightened demand for these grain varieties among the populace. Consequently, the *kardars* found it convenient to sell these at elevated prices, exceeding by far those prescribed by the government.

4. ***Mokuddum***: At the village level, the *mokuddums* assumed the responsibility for detecting anomalies or thefts, facilitating the recruitment of labour and transport for governmental or other purposes as well as maintaining comprehensive records of the village's agricultural produce. This duty was jointly discharged with another functionary, designated as the *patwaree*.

5. ***Patwaree***: Specialising in maintaining discrete accounts for each *zamindar's* domicile within the village, the *patwaree* meticulously documented diverse crops linked to each property. This position was mandatory for the *zamindars* to employ, as they were responsible for tax collection. *Patwarees* were remunerated by the *zamindars* and typically represented the Pundit community.

6. ***Shugdur***: In numbers ranging from one to four per village contingent on its size, the *shugdur*s were tasked with monitoring crops in situ, as well as overseeing the government's portion post-harvest, awaiting transfer to state storage facilities. Instances of oppression were purported, where the *shugdur*s coerced monetary concessions from the *zamindars*, leveraging the threat of accusing them of pilfering government grain. Faced with the prospect of investigations, the *zamindars* commonly resorted to compensatory settlements commensurate with their capacity. The *shugdurs* were also often provided with receipts without charge.

7. ***Sargowl***: This official assumed oversight of the *shugdur*s, typically numbering one *sargowl* per every ten villages. Responsibilities encompassed supervisory checks on the *shugdur*s, with subsequent reporting to their respective *kardars*.

Reports suggested that the *sargowls* frequently extorted money from the *shugdur*s via methods akin to those employed by the *shugdur*s against the *zamindar*s. Strikingly, those subjected to such oppression seldom contemplated reporting such grievances to higher echelons of authority, reflecting diminished faith in the impartiality of officials, notwithstanding their ostensible responsibility to address the complaints. The *sargowls* often hailed from the Hindu community as was the case with the Dogra administration at various levels at the time.

8. **Taroughdar**: Their role was primarily vested in assessing the weight of grain during the extraction of the government's allotment from the *zamindar*s. The *taroughdar*s consistently accompanied the *kardar*s during these proceedings.
9. **Hurkara**: Equivalent of a police constable, each *hurkara* was allocated a realm encompassing roughly twenty villages. All male members of their family played the roles of *hurkara*s.
10. **Doom**: Representing a local policeman at the village level, *doom*s were supplied with *russeed* by inhabitants of their respective localities. They liaised with and were directed by *hurkara*s.

The Kashmir landowning class assumed the responsibility of supporting a relatively modest official apparatus, a major part of which was necessitated by the intricate administrative framework underpinning the collection of agricultural produce. Aligned with local practices, land ownership followed a communal pattern, obligating the village's *patwaree* (record keeper) to meticulously record the discrete yield of each crop affiliated with individual dwellings. Subsequent calculations entailed determining the quantum owed to the government based on the ensuing metric, which will be elucidated in due course. Kashmir's agricultural taxonomy, in a manner akin to that in the rest of India, bifurcated crops into *rubbia* and *khareefa* categories. *Rubbia* pertains to those maturing around

July, while *khareefa* encompasses crops reaped approximately two months thereafter. Except rice, all *khareefa* crops constituted second harvests, sourced from land where rice was cultivated previously. Rice was exclusively sown between May and September.

The government's standardised weight metrics used in its grain apportionment were as follows:

6 *seers* = 1 *trak*
16 *traks* = 1 *kharwah*

However, when the grain is distributed to the populace, the scaling shifted to:

6 *seers* = 1 *trak*
15 *traks* = 1 *kharwah*

This variance led to an additional *trak* accruing to the government within each *kharwah*, intended to defray the expenses associated with grain transportation from villages to the city. Given the favourable terms of carriage compensation provided by the government, this supplementary allotment was considered amply adequate.

In conjunction with the *rubbia* and *khareefa* crops, the government and its affiliated officials requisitioned the portions below from the *zamindars* (landowners).

From every 32 *traks* of *rubbia* crop grain, the following quantities were claimed:

Government share: 20 *traks* 0 seer
Surgowl: 0 *traks* 1.5 seer
Shugdur: 0 *traks* 1 seer
Taroughdar: 0 *traks* ¾ seer
Hurkara: 0 *traks* 1.5 seer
Patwaree: 0 *traks* 1.5 seer
Servants of the *Kardar*: 0 *traks* 0.5 seer

An analysis of the deductions made from the yield of agricultural produce in Kashmir presents a complex system of taxation, encompassing both in-kind collections and monetary impositions, and thereby reveals the multifaceted economic dynamics inherent in the region's agricultural landscape. This system, intricately tied to the structure of land revenue collection, supported a network of officials engaged in the administration and management of these levies.

The *rubbia* crop, comprising diverse grains, underwent deductions for governmental and administrative purposes. These deductions included both in-kind appropriations and monetary impositions. The *rubbia* grains such as *kunuck, uiska, kurre, tilogogole, kuttan, marhar, mong, mosour* and *krotur* bore specific monetary levies corresponding to every set of 32 *traks* of their yield. These levies, measured in *Chilkee* annas, served as additional fiscal obligations alongside the in-kind deductions.

Similar to the *rubbia* crop, the *khareefa* crop also faced a comprehensive system of deductions. These deductions, rooted in both in-kind collections and monetary levies, are administered to grains such as *shalee, mukki, trombu, shawul* and *kapa*s. These levies were articulated in terms of Chilkee annas and were appended to the yield of every set of 32 *trak*s of the *khareefa* crop.

In addition to the crop-related deductions mentioned above, Kashmir's fiscal landscape comprised a spectrum of auxiliary taxes and levies. The *russo-dart* tax, imposed annually on households, followed a graduated scale based on the number of inhabitants. Moreover, the fruit tax pertained to profitable fruit crops, including walnuts, apples, pears, apricots, almonds and quinces, where a substantial portion of the annual yield was appropriated by the government. Furthermore, there was a distinct array of taxes on animals such as sheep, goats and ponies, and on products such as ghee, poultry and honey.

As discussed earlier, the *patwaree* and *mokuddum* held the responsibility of maintaining accounts and managing the distribution of the returned funds. This exemplifies the Kashmir region's intricate and elaborate economic and administrative structure, intertwined with the economic fabric of Kashmir and embodied by its hierarchy of officials. This facilitated the implementation of a comprehensive taxation system, involving a nuanced interplay of crop-related in-kind collections and auxiliary monetary levies, as described before. This in turn enabled multidimensional management of the region's agricultural and fiscal systems.

The aforementioned delineation applied to the taxation regimen imposed upon the agrarian proprietors within the region of Kashmir, comprising the rural populace while excluding the urban inhabitants situated within prominent towns such as Srinagar, Anantnag (also called Islamabad by locals), Sopore and Pampore. It is imperative to underscore that these levies, comprising both pecuniary and in-kind requisitions emanating from the *rubbia* and *khareefa* harvests, were sanctioned within the official domain of government taxes rather than unauthorised exactions orchestrated by governmental officials.

Under these circumstances where legitimate grievances surfaced, and presuming the *thanedar* remained impervious to the inducements of the *kardar*, redress was attainable through a monetary outlay ranging between one and two rupees, accompanied by the concomitant loss of temporal resources. However, the alternative scenario, wherein the *thanedar* fell for the allurements of monetary incentives, made the aggrieved landowner invoke the higher authority by recourse to the tehsildar. This kind of redress was fraught with potential for pre-emptive circumvention engendered by collusion between the *kardar* and the *thanedar*, thereby prompting the landowner to acquiesce to fiscal diminution and go for compromise.

The ramifications of these systemic lacunae manifested in the domain of trade and commercial interchange between the rural and urban strata. The urban populace, comprising of merchants, shawl traders, artisans, and sundry practitioners, evinced a demand for agricultural staples including rice, corn, poultry, and dairy products. Conversely, the rural landowners harboured a reciprocal demand for currency to facilitate their acquisition of imported commodities that emanated from the urban centres. This inherently symbiotic pattern of exchange, however, was effectively stifled by the existing framework. This induced circumstances–as corroborated even by reliable English sources–where urban residents, while possessing currency, confronted extremely difficult living conditions. The urban requisition for agricultural yield found itself in a state of steady decline due to the pervasive scarcity of surplus provisions, which was further exacerbated by the intermittent closure of the government *kotas* or granaries.

Later regulatory measures, which facilitated the acquisition of essential quantity of grain from the government, afforded a modicum of respite. This modest provision had been met with expressions of gratitude within the Kashmir populace. Evidentiary support for the gratitude was garnered from the burgeoning attendance at community gatherings marked by elevated participation, attributable to this newfound accessibility to sustenance. The conspicuous appreciation for this provision underscored the disquieting impact of the prevalent oppression and maltreatment on the common people of Kashmir.

It is incumbent upon us to recognise that the land produce taxation system in place was far from novel in inception, as its origin can be traced to epochs predating the Dogra regime. Nevertheless, there was a salient point of divergence in the valuations of grain transactions conducted through the mechanism of government *kotas*. During the inauguration of Gulab Singh's reign, the taxation apparatus bore marked semblance to the pre-existing schemes described here, albeit with significant differences. The rates governing the procurement of grain via government kotas during his regime were as follows:

Shalee (unprocessed rice) - 1 HS Rupee per Kharwah
Uiska (barley) - 1 HS Rupee per Kharwah
Mukki (Indian corn) - 1 HS Rupee per Kharwah
Oil - 1 HS Rupee per Kharwah
and commensurate proportions for other grains
(1 Huree Singh (HS) Rupee = 8 Annas)

Eventually, when a landowner endeavoured to contest an excessive levy, based on the intricate scale expounded earlier, he sought the help of the *thanedar* overseeing their *purgunnah*. This would trigger an investigative trajectory culminating in the summoning of the *kardar* and p*atwaree* for a requisite inquiry.

In the annals of monetary reform, Gulab Singh's reign witnessed a notable alteration in the coinage. Correspondingly, this epoch marked an elevation in the cost of government-conducted transactions, surpassing existing valuations that had been revised during his tenure. Enumerated thus, the prevailing prices were as follows:

Shalee - 2 Ch Rs per Kharwah
Kunuck - 5 Ch Rs per Kharwah
Makki - 2 Ch Rs per Kharwah
Muttur (peas) - 4 Ch Rs per Kharwah
Moong (a staple dal) - 7 Ch Rs per Kharwah
Mohar - 7 Ch Rs per Kharwah
Mosoor - 4 Ch Rs per Kharwah

Krotur - 2 Ch Rs per Kharwah
Kuttum (source of oil) - 6 Ch Rs per Kharwah
Mout (cattle fodder) - 2 Ch Rs per Kharwah
Tilogogolo (source of oil) - 8 Ch Rs per Kharwah
Tromba (buckwheat) - 2 Ch Rs per Kharwah
Pingi (grains used as food by the Showul populace)
- 2 Ch Rs per Kharwah
Kupas (flax) - 16 Ch Rs per Kharwah
(1 Chikee Rupee (Ch Rs) = 10 Annas)

In effect, these price escalations resulted in doubling the previous prices, supplanting the tariffs prevalent at the time of Gulab Singh's assumption of administrative control. It was pertinent, furthermore, to address the implausible contention that the system's longevity merited its defence, when in reality it contained inherent deficiencies. Central to this financial modality were the government *kotas*, serving as repositories for grain stores and simultaneously offering provisions to the populace in modest allotments.

Entities requiring larger quantities of provisions necessarily needed to liaise with the custodian of the *kotas*, who in turn furnished an endorsement to a designated *kardar*. In effecting this transaction, remuneration was paid and subsequently accounted for within the *kardar*'s records. However, grain commodities from the government *kotas* were often of deficient quality attributable to decomposition en route from rural environs. It is worth noting here that the government's *kharwah*, when used for selling to the public, stood at a count of 15 *trak*s, lower than the standard 16 *trak*s.

A major line of activity connected with this fiscal framework comprised deliberate impeding of commercial intercourse between urban and rural spheres – a nexus crucial for ensuring long-term communal welfare. The subsequent ramifications included the precipitous destitution among the *zamindar* class and the palpable adversity borne by the shawl weaver and *sada-baf* segments. Additionally, the administrative latitude exercised by the government and its functionaries engendered strong potential for engineered scarcities via strategic closure of government *kotas*, thus ineluctably inflating grain valuations. Lastly, such complex modus operandi of this fiscal edifice made manifold opportunities available to local functionaries for machination and exploitation.

Resultantly, the atrophy of cross-sectional interchange and transaction that this system propagated was instrumental in nurturing a palpable sentiment of mutual scepticism and jealousy between urban and agrarian constituents, profoundly compromising the holistic well-being of the society. Evidently, within the purview of a Machiavellian administration akin to that of Jammu, the preservation of such a milieu appeared as a strategic objective, rather than its amelioration.

Robert Thorp believed that such cognitive inertia was equivalent to complicity and doubted whether the Maharajah even cared minimally for his subjects' welfare. Throp was critical of the Maharaja's dependence on reports from his officials and his infrequent visits to the Kashmir valley, noting that he preferred to stay in the luxurious palace in Jammu. The Maharaja was not very receptive to criticism of his economic policies, mainly due to his unwavering reliance on intermediaries like the *dihwans* and *wuzeers*. For all practical purposes, there was a disconnect between the echelons of Kashmir's administrative elite and its populace. The relationship between the two was one marked by 'deep-seated animosities and incommensurate polarities between its Muslim and Hindu constituents'. This perennial antithesis, in which Muslims and Hindus are principal constituents, engenders a milieu wherein a nation of almost exclusively

Muslim populace is beholden to a governing apparatus dominated by adherents of the Hindu faith.

Developmental Work in Kashmir during the Mughal Period

During the Mughal period, Kashmir witnessed the developmental progress outlined below:

1. **Agricultural Development:** During the period of Mughal dominion, Kashmir underwent a noteworthy surge in agricultural development, resulting in the evolution of the region into a flourishing agrarian society. This transformative process was contingent upon strategic initiatives and interventions systematically implemented by the Mughal administration.

    (a) **Expansion of Cultivated Land:** Preceding Mughal intervention, extensive expanses of land in Kashmir lay fallow or were underutilised. Recognising the agricultural potential of the valley, the Mughals launched a meticulously planned campaign to augment cultivated land. This endeavour encompassed the issuance of land rights, provision of incentives to farmers, and the establishment of safeguards against local conflicts, collectively culminating in heightened agricultural productivity.

    (b) **Introduction of New Crops and Farming Techniques**: The Mughals introduced a diverse array of crops, diversifying the agrarian landscape of the region. The ascendancy of rice, now a staple in Kashmir, owes its prominence to this epoch. Additionally, agricultural practices from disparate regions of the Mughal Empire, inclusive of crop rotation and refined irrigation methodologies, were introduced, thereby fostering enhanced yields.

    (c) **Systematic Revenue Collection and Land Measurement**: The reign of Akbar witnessed the implementation of the *Zabt* system, introducing a standardised approach to revenue collection. This meticulous system relied extensively on precise land measurements, with designated officials, referred to as *'patwaris* (or *patwarees*) entrusted with the task of land measurement and record maintenance. Such systematic measures ensured equitable taxation, fostering a climate of trust between the farming community and the administrative apparatus.

(d) **Irrigation Projects:** Despite the inherent advantage of abundant rivers and lakes in Kashmir, the region's agricultural potential was not fully harnessed until the Mughals embarked upon extensive irrigation initiatives. This entailed the construction of canals and diversion of waterways to ensure equitable distribution of water to even the remotest fields. The result was a consistent and prolific harvest, impervious to the caprices of weather fluctuations.

The cumulative consequence of these multifaceted developments was momentous. The erstwhile sporadic agricultural undertakings in the valley underwent a metamorphosis into a robust and systematically organised sector under the aegis of Mughal governance. Improved agricultural yields translated into augmented state revenues, and Kashmir, as an integral entity, reaped the dividends of a thriving agrarian economy.

2. **Craft and Industry**: The Mughal epoch, characterised not only by political and administrative progression but also by a pronounced cultural and artistic efflorescence, engendered transformative developments in the craft and industry sectors of Kashmir. This period witnessed the emergence of Kashmiri handicrafts as an intrinsic component of the region's identity and economic framework, fostered by Mughal patronage.

(a) **Pashmina Shawl Industry:** Among these artisanal

endeavours, the Pashmina shawl industry stood out as a marker of Kashmiri identity. Renowned for their soft texture and intricate designs, Pashmina shawls became coveted luxury items within the Mughal Empire and found markets in Central Asia and Europe. These shawls manifested the artistic acumen of Kashmiri craftsmen. The proclivity of Mughal emperors, notably Jahangir and his successors, to be portrayed adorned in these shawls in paintings underscored their importance for the Mughals and advertised these products far and wide.

(b) **Carpet Weaving, Papier-Mâché, and Silk Production:** Various other crafts also experienced heightened prominence under Mughal patronage. Carpet weaving, drawing inspiration from Persian motifs and techniques, attained a zenith of significance, symbolising both luxury and artistic finesse. The art of papier-mâché, involving intricate designs on moulded paper pulp, flourished, giving rise to an array of decorative items such as vases and jewellery boxes. Simultaneously, the sericulture industry prospered, augmenting the multifaceted repertoire of Kashmiri craftsmanship.

(c) **Development of Saffron Cultivation**: The indigenous saffron cultivation in Kashmir, which was there before the Mughals brought Kashmir under their control, experienced substantial growth during this era. Geographical regions endowed with conducive climates and fertile soils, particularly Pampore, emerged as centres for saffron cultivation. The growing popularity of saffron, because of its aroma and perceived medicinal properties, contributed significantly to the local economy.

(d) **Promotion of Handicrafts and Arts:** Mughal emperor Jahangir had a personal predilection towards the arts and crafts, which played a critical role in their institutional promotion. Royal patronage provided economic sustenance to artisans and afforded them a platform for the exhibition and commercialisation of their creations. This confluence of Mughal patronage and artisanal dexterity elevated Kashmiri handicrafts to unforeseen levels of excellence.

In sum, there was a renaissance in the field of crafts and industries in Kashmir under the Mughals. The enduring legacy of this era is palpable even in the contemporary global market, where Kashmiri handicrafts continue to be valued and admired as emblems of artisanal brilliance.

Developmental Works in Kashmir during the Afghan Period

The Afghan rule in Kashmir, spanning a period of 67 years, was characterised by some notable developmental initiatives under the governance of 4 Pathan emperors at the Afghan Imperial court and approximately 26 governors in the Kashmir province. In terms of administrative evolution, the Afghan administration in Kashmir seamlessly extended and built upon the foundations laid by the Mughal administrative machinery, introducing strategic changes to enhance the efficiency of governance. Rather than undertaking a complete overhaul of administrative measures in the valley, the Afghan rulers focused on continuing and, in certain cases, refining the systems initiated by the early Mughals. While preserving the essence of governance structures, they brought about specific modifications, particularly in revenue administration, which will be discussed in detail later. Nomenclatural changes were implemented under the Afghan administration, exemplified by the shift from *karguzar* (the official name of *naib subadar* under the Mughals) to *sahibkar*. This transition reflected a conscious effort to adapt and modernise administrative designations.

Amidst these developments, the role of the *subadar* emerged as pivotal, showcasing visible transformation and serving as the immediate representative of central authority. The *subadar* played a crucial role in maintaining law and order in the province and facilitating the streamlined transport of revenue from various *purgunnahs* (or *parganas*) to the imperial court. The military commanders, often entrusted with the responsibility of *subadar*ship, contributed to the consolidation of territories and the suppression of rebellions, fostering stability and progress.

Contrary to the conventional replacement of subadars based on stipulated timeframes, the Afghan rule witnessed changes in *subadars* either in response to revolts against imperial authority or due to complaints from their subordinates in the imperial court. An illustrative example is the written complaint lodged by Amir Khan Sher Jawan against the inefficiency of the *subadar*, Khuram Khan, resulting in the replacement of the latter by Amir Khan Sher Jawan. In the context of Kashmir, subadars retained their positions as long as they remained in the favour of the emperor, devoid of any specific tenure allocation. The tenure of Afghan *subadars* in Kashmir exhibited a diverse pattern, with certain governors administering the territory for only a few months and others leading provinces for several years.

The very first *subadar*, Abdullah Khan Ishaq Aqsai, ruled for a brief six months before appointing Khawaja Abdul Khan Kabuli, initiating a chain of subsequent subadars with varying tenures. Some *subadars* such as Raja Sukh Jiwan Mal, Amir Khan Sher Jawan, Haji Karim Dad, Sardar Abdullah Khan, Atta Mohammad Khan and Wazir Mohammad Khan had notable administrative tenures ranging from six and a half years to eleven years. Distinct from the Mughal administration, where significant positions were directly appointed by the emperor, the Afghan *subadars* assumed the responsibility of appointing officials for crucial provincial positions such as *nazim/subadar, sahibkar, peshkar, diwan, qazi, qari* and others. This provision allowed each *subadar* to select officials for these subordinate roles upon their appointment. The appointment mechanism was initiated by the first governor, Ishaq Aqsai, who, before departing for Kabul, appointed Khawaja Abdullah Khan as the new *subadar* of Kashmir along with his *sahibkar* Sukh Jiwan Mal in 1752. Subsequent *subadars* continued this practice, appointing officials to key positions during their tenures.

This empowerment of *subadars* in the appointment of officials extended beyond *sahibkari*, encompassing most other positions in the provincial court. Notably, the authority to appoint immediate subordinates provided *subadars* with the autonomy to select either their kin or their friends for several significant positions in administration. While *subadars* gradually became influential and capable of initiating or diluting institutions as per their political and vested interests, this autonomy did not always lead to rebellion against imperial authority. Instead, it fostered a more nuanced dynamic, with *subadars* occasionally proclaiming themselves as independent rulers or aligning with regional kingdoms.

Out of 26 Afghan governors, 11 *subadars* took up arms against Afghan authority, either declaring themselves independent rulers or affiliating with other regional kingdoms. The first Afghan governor attempting to separate Kashmir from the Afghan empire was Sukh Jiwan Mal.[30] Additionally, *subadars* such as Mir Faqir Kanth, Amir Khan Sher Jawan, Azad Khan and Mir Hazar Khan attempted to separate Kashmir from Afghan rule, albeit failing to establish a permanent independent government. Despite not introducing a distinct political organisation, the Afghan rulers integrated additional functionaries, particularly in revenue administration, to enhance efficiency in revenue collection. One notable addition was the introduction of the *peshkar* office in Kashmir, primarily dealing with revenue and custom affairs. This office played a crucial role in economic matters, acting as a personal assistant to the subadar.

The introduction of the *peshkar* office, alongside the roles of *sahibkar* and *peshkar*, showcased the Afghan rulers' commitment to developing and optimising administrative structures for better governance. The roles of these offices were delineated, with *sahibkar* assisting in maintaining law and order and *peshkar* primarily focusing on economic affairs. However, these positions were occasionally held by the same official, demonstrating flexibility in the administrative approach. In summary, the Afghan rule in Kashmir, spanning over nearly seven decades, was characterised by developmental efforts that built upon the existing Mughal administrative framework. The Afghan rulers demonstrated adaptability and innovation, bringing about changes in nomenclature, empowering *subadars* in the appointment of officials, and introducing additional functionaries to enhance revenue administration. The nuanced dynamics between imperial authority and *subadars* resulted in a blend of stability and occasional attempts at autonomy, contributing to the historical tapestry of Kashmir during the Afghan rule.

Developmental Works in Kashmir during the Dogra Period

After the Afghan era, Kashmir came under Dogra rule. During this period, its economy relied primarily on agriculture. The Dogra period saw the emergence of key textile sectors in Kashmir, including shawls, silk, and carpets. The artisanal shawl industry of the 19th century played a crucial role in shaping the economic landscape of the valley.[31] By 1860, shawl production became a central aspect of Kashmir's export trade, witnessing increased demand from markets in Persia, Turkey, Europe, and America. The economic significance of the shawl industry is evident through the establishment of the Department of Industries in 1923, the Jammu and Kashmir State Marketing Board in 1935 and the Jammu and Kashmir Bank in 1937-38. However, A Gani (1990) argues that these initiatives were unsuccessful in improving the state's industrial structure, as they were seen as serving British interests. Consequently, consumers rejected them.[32] The importance of the shawl industry is further highlighted by statistics from 1863, indicating 23,013 shawl weavers in Kashmir generating an average annual income of seven lakh rupees from shawls between 1846 and 1863[33] Srinagar became the focal point of textile craftsmanship, as noted by Frederic Drew in the 1860s and 1870s, with a significant population of shawl weavers contributing to Kashmir's reputation in India and Europe.

During Gulab Singh's reign, shawl weavers endured dire conditions, as they were restricted by laws preventing them from changing employers. Half of their modest daily wage of four annas was claimed in taxes, and the remaining two annas were compensated in kind (paddy) at inflated rates from government depots. The shawl industry encountered setbacks in the late 19th century due to heavy government taxes, the repercussions of the Franco–German War of 1870 on shawl production, and the competition posed by machine-made imitation shawls abroad. In the latter part of the 19th century, silk supplanted shawls in Kashmir's export economy. Sericulture, under state control, burgeoned into a dominant industry, with the Srinagar Silk Factory evolving into the world's largest within two decades. By 1905, Kashmiri silk dominated the European market due to its superior quality compared to

Bengal silk.[34] However, after 1913, the industry encountered setbacks, including a devastating fire at the Srinagar Silk Factory and the disruptions caused by the outbreak of World War I in 1914, leading to the closure of European markets (Britain and France). The Dogra administration implemented various measures for industrial development, exemplified by the establishment of the Department of Industries in 1923.

Post-Dogra Rule

Following the termination of Dogra rule, the geopolitical landscape of Kashmir underwent a transformative phase, marked by its emergence as a contested territory between India and Pakistan. Jammu and Kashmir, while remaining under the jurisdiction of the Union of India, witnessed a forced annexation of roughly a third of Jammu and Kashmir by Pakistan, effectively isolating it from the broader Kashmir region. The ensuing disparities in developmental trajectories between the parts under Indian and Pakistani control have become pronounced, with the former experiencing notable advancements in stark contrast to the latter, which appears to be subjected to a quasi-colonial status, characterised by a dearth of visible progress. The residents of Pakistan Occupied Kashmir (PoK) find themselves constrained in expressing political and socio-economic grievances, a circumstance contributing to underdevelopment and disenfranchisement. The evident lack of robust educational institutions, healthcare facilities, and gainful employment opportunities compels a substantial portion of PoK's populace to seek menial employment in either the urban centres of Pakistan or in the Gulf countries. Official statistics from PoK's planning and development department reveal substantial deficits in access to basic amenities, as exemplified by a 50 per cent population lacking piped water and a staggering 78 per cent of households devoid of tap water connections. Healthcare provision in PoK falls below accepted Pakistani standards, evident in elevated population-to-doctor ratios compared to mainland Pakistan and an elevated infant mortality rate relative to the national average. The dearth of significant industries in the region is attributed to Islamabad's neglect of local investment and redirecting its focus toward utilising PoK land for training camps and launch pads for various terrorist organisations, notably the Punjabi Taliban network.

In contradistinction, the Union Territory of Jammu and Kashmir has emerged as an exemplar of successful development, owing to the infusion of substantial financial resources from New Delhi. Since the abrogation of its special status and its transition into a Union Territory, Jammu and Kashmir has witnessed commendable progress. The allocation of funds by the central government is executed impartially for the collective welfare of all residents, indicative of a commitment to equitable development. Prospective investments in Jammu and Kashmir, identified by global investors as a region with significant untapped potential, have come to fruition through formal agreements, including one signed at the Dubai Expo 2020. These agreements underscore the region's prospects for sustained economic growth and development, serving as a poignant illustration of the disparately contrasting developmental trajectories within the broader Kashmir region.

Chapter II
J&K in India (1947-1989)
Beginning of a Saga of Development

THE ACCESSION of the princely state of J&K to India took place on 26 October 1947. Following the accession, the relationship between the State and the Union was cemented on the basis of special provisions under the broader ambit of the terms of the Instrument of Accession. The accession was subsequently formalised through the constitutional provision of Article 370. Even as the state retained a considerable amount of authority in internal matters, its financial dependence on New Delhi increased gradually over the years.

In the immediate aftermath of the accession of J&K to India, its comprehensive integration with the Union of India emerged as a focal point. This required concerted efforts on the part of New Delhi to smoothen the process. The stabilisation of the region and the addressing of its security concerns became paramount in the light of the Pakistan-sponsored aggression on J&K (tribal invasion in October 1947 and the protracted war till the ceasefire of 31 December 1948) in order to forcefully annex it. These developments raised a new challenge that involved guarding the de facto border between India and Pakistan in J&K–and the Cease-fire Line (CFL) finalised on 27 July 1949. This eventually became the Line of Control (LoC) with minor modifications, after the 1971 war, specifically in

July 1972. This made it necessary to redirect a major proportion of monetary and material resources towards completing crucial infrastructure projects, such as roads and communication networks, for safeguarding the country's sovereignty and at the same time, extending the developmental framework adopted by the Indian leadership to J&K.

With J&K hosting a substantial number of refugees from Pakistan and Pakistan-occupied Jammu and Kashmir (PoJK), the Central Government's financial allocations for the state included provisions to address this challenge by supporting the relief and rehabilitation efforts in the state. This encompassed providing essential items such as shelter, food and medical aid to the large numbers of refugees and displaced persons, who had been affected by the Partition. The aim was to alleviate the immediate humanitarian crisis and facilitate the resettlement of those affected.

As such, these events influenced the Central Government's decisions to sanction generous financial aid to stabilise the region, not only by addressing its security concerns but also by formalising its economy and helping to take care of its infrastructural requirements.[35] This played a vital role in shaping the region's developmental trajectory before the Pakistan-sponsored armed insurgency halted it in the late 1980s. Yet these resources appeared inadequate for raising the necessary level of infrastructure in the state, including expanding its industrial base to broaden the economic avenues. In this context, this chapter attempts to provide a detailed account and a comprehensive analysis of the monetary allocations made by the Central Government to J&K right from India's Independence in 1947 to the onset of terrorism in 1989. It further attempts to map out the primary trends, priorities and challenges that the state encountered in its journey towards achieving economic and infrastructural objectives in this period.

J&K's Economic Development: Humble Beginnings (1950-1960)

Within three years of the end of British rule in the country, the foundation of modern India was laid by Prime Minister Jawaharlal Nehru and his colleagues. It included unveiling both short-term and long-term measures, highlighted by the initiation of Five Year Plans (FYPs) to steer the country towards economic prosperity and modernisation. As noted above and in the preceding chapters, J&K's relationship with the Union of India was formalised under Article 370 in the early 1950s, granting the state a degree of autonomy in internal matters, including its fiscal matters.[36]

This substantial degree of fiscal autonomy enabled J&K to manage its finances independent of the Central Government's oversight to some extent. The state retained flexibility to tailor its economic and fiscal policies according to its specific needs and priorities. The distinct status underscored the special considerations and recognition given to the unique circumstances of J&K and played a crucial role in shaping the state's economic policies and priorities during this time.

This distinctiveness of the state was also shaped by the pro-people measures adopted by the state's first elected government (even though most of the members of the first legislative assembly were elected unopposed), under the leadership of Sheikh Abdullah, which embraced the developmental ethos advocated by Prime Minister Nehru. Sheikh Abdullah, a crusader against the state's pre-accession feudalism under the Dogra dynasty, which had disadvantaged the majority peasant class for over a century, pursued an ambitious programme of radical land reforms as one of its primary policy initiatives to drive the development of the state (see Table 2.1).

Sheikh Abdullah, the most popular leader of Jammu and Kashmir at the time, had earlier come out with his famous memorandum demanding far-ranging economic and political reforms. He had presented this memorandum to Maharaja Hari Singh and it contained a detailed economic plan in 1939. It had become famous as the 'Naya Kashmir' document. After assuming power, the Kashmiri leadership conducted its affairs as per the principles proposed in this document. This culminated in the enactment of the 'Big Landed Estates Abolition Act' in 1950, which effectuated the transfer of land ownership to cultivators without affording any compensation to the erstwhile landlords.[37] A statutory ceiling on general landholding to 22.75 acres was implemented. This legislation requisitioned in excess of 8,00,000 acres of land from 8,989 landowners, of which the rights to approximately 2,47,000 acres were subsequently redistributed to approximately 2,00,000 farming households.

Table 2.1 Key developments and legislation

Year	Key Developments and Legislation
1947	State government under Sheikh Abdullah adopts a socialist development ideology.
1950	Big Landed Estates Abolition Act redistributes land to cultivators without compensating landlords; imposes a general ceiling of 22 3/4 acres.
1976	Agrarian Reform Act introduces a standard ceiling of 12.5 acres for orchards.

Despite this, the early 1950s also marked J&K's integration into the modernisation and development planning process of India, with the Central Government extending generous financial provisions to help the state navigate any challenges whatsoever.[38] For instance, the Central Government reduced J&K's fiscal obligations amounting to Rs 1.75 crores to Rs 85 lakhs via the enactment of the Distressed Debt Relief Act, while further extinguishing mortgage debts to the tune of Rs 14.38 lakhs.[39]

The introduction of Five-Year Plans became instrumental in channelling financial resources towards various development projects across the state. These projects spanned multiple sectors including agriculture, industry, education and healthcare. The incorporation of Jammu and Kashmir into the broader national development strategy signified a concerted effort to foster comprehensive growth and address the diverse needs of the population.

As such, the 1950s marked a crucial period for Jammu and Kashmir, characterised by a shift towards long-term economic development and modernisation. The infusion of financial support, the integration into national planning processes, and the grant of special autonomous status were instrumental in shaping the trajectory of the state's economic and developmental endeavours during this transformative era.

The aforementioned land reforms had profound repercussions for the rural economic landscape. A transformative alteration in landholding patterns transpired over the subsequent four decades, transitioning from a landscape characterised predominantly by extensive landholdings to one marked by diminishing land sizes. In 1953, 42 per cent of landholdings were observed to encompass areas of less than one hectare, collectively constituting a mere 14 per cent of the total land mass. By the year 1986, an overwhelming 73 per cent of the total number of holdings were within the 0–1-hectare range, comprising 32 per cent of the total land area. The transformation was also confirmed by a corresponding decline in the prevalence of large landholdings (exceeding 4 hectares), from constituting 6 per cent of the total holdings and 22 per cent of the aggregate land area in 1953 to a diminutive 2 per cent of the total holdings and 16 per cent of the overall land area by 1986. This shift, while engendering a heightened sense of equity and social justice, simultaneously engendered a situation characterised by pronounced land fragmentation and parcelisation, with the average farm size descending substantially below the nationally accepted optimal dimensions for agricultural endeavours in India.

In the context of Kashmir, the typical landholding is now conspicuously minuscule, standing at a mere 0.99 hectares in stark contrast to the national average of 1.82 hectares. The upshot of such intense fragmentation has been observed to exert a detrimental influence on agricultural productivity, particularly in regions characterised by terrain variations where distinct parcels of land are distributed between valley floors and hilly terrains without access to irrigation. This has constricted the scope for the widespread adoption of modernised production techniques and efficient fertilizer utilization. Notably, in 1987, the state of Kashmir registered a meagre fertilizer consumption rate of 30 kg per hectare, significantly below the national average of 50 kg per hectare.

Uneven Pace: Attempts to Expand from Agro-dominance (1960-1970)

By the mid-1960s, institutional transformation through the medium of land reform had faltered in its endeavour to revolutionise the agricultural landscape, as the state endured food shortages. This failure was primarily attributable to the manoeuvrings of the rural oligarchy, which orchestrated these changes in a manner that predominantly advanced their interests. Consequently, a fundamental shift in the state's approach was undertaken, advocating a fresh approach that underscored technological modernisation as the principal route to heightened productivity within the newly established small-scale farming units.

In the year 1976, the legislative machinery was once again

set into motion with the introduction of yet another pivotal legislation–the 'Agrarian Reform Act'. This piece of legislation, in pursuit of extirpating the vestiges of landlord-tenant relations, introduced a standardised ceiling of 12.5 acres for orchards. Given the complexity and implications of these legal reforms, it becomes apparent that in-depth field studies are an imperative, as they offer the potential to furnish a comprehensive assessment of the nuanced phenomenon termed 'neo-landlordism' within the socio-economic fabric of Kashmir.

Various policy instruments were instituted to rectify systemic inadequacies within factor and commodity markets, with the overarching aim of elevating agricultural output. This recalibration in approach resonates with the conceptual framework articulated by T. N. Srinivasan,[40] in his oft-cited article on economic development in a state in the framework of neoclassical economy, wherein a benevolent state meticulously deploys appropriate policy mechanisms to exert effective intervention.[41] The new approach included the adoption of innovative techniques such as institutional finance, the establishment of a public delivery system, the implementation of a responsive pricing mechanism, and the diversification of commodity markets. Notably, the Intensive Agricultural District Programme and High Yielding Varieties Programme, initiated during the 1960s, yielded discernible positive outcomes, particularly manifest in the form of elevated crop yields spanning food and non-food crops, including paddy, wheat, maize and apples. These agricultural interventions were further bolstered by extensive public expenditure on subsidies earmarked for rural development within Kashmir.

While efforts took place to streamline J&K's agriculture sector to accord a modicum of food subsistence in the state, the Central Government encouraged attention towards other sectors of the state. It included refurbishing the region's nascent infrastructure through increased allocations towards enhancing transport connectivity, while marketing Kashmir as a prime tourist destination in the country. These initiatives aimed to bolster the region's economic prospects and establish a sustainable foundation for growth.

In terms of infrastructure development, notable efforts were made in developing basic infrastructure such as roads and bridges, symbolised by projects such as elevation of the Jammu–Srinagar cart road into a National Highway. This was highlighted by the construction of the Jawahar Tunnel, in a highly difficult topography laced with geological fault lines, to circumvent the mighty Banihal Pass. This underscored the Central Government's resolve to bring development to the state and connect it to the Indian mainland. The highway has since become a crucial transportation artery for J&K, not only facilitating better connectivity within the state but also playing a pivotal role in promoting trade, tourism and overall economic development.

Parallel to the government's efforts to allocate financial provisions for raising basic infrastructure, the decade of the 1960s also witnessed a dedicated effort towards the promotion of tourism in Jammu and Kashmir.[42] Substantial financial allocations were directed towards the development of key tourist destinations, with a specific focus on enhancing the appeal of places such as Dal Lake, Gulmarg and Pahalgam. The picturesque landscapes, serene lakes and snow-capped mountains were actively marketed to attract tourists, especially from outside the country. This concerted push resulted in J&K becoming a popular tourist destination for both domestic and foreign visitors.[43] The region's appeal was further enhanced by the Central Government encouraging Bollywood filmmakers to harness Kashmir's natural landscape for film shootings, resulting in blockbusters such as *Kashmir Ki Kali*, helping market it as the romance capital of India. These efforts had a lasting impact on the tourism industry, establishing the state as a sought-after destination for travellers seeking tranquillity and natural splendour.

However, the state continued facing challenges on its borders such as Chinese aggression in 1962 in the Ladakh region on the eastern front and Pakistani aggression in 1965 on the western front. This influenced governmental decisions to make added allocations to tackle these challenges and secure the borders, including enhancing border road connectivity.

Nevertheless, in the 1960s, the Central Government's liberal financial allocations were not only aimed at enhancing the state's connectivity and accessibility, but also towards positioning it as a prominent tourist destination and thereby ensuring its contribution to the socio-economic upliftment of the region.

Towards Political Turmoil and Developmental Path (1970-1989)

Even though the Central Government continued to make generous financial allocations to the state, the state continued to witness challenges. Infrastructure development, in particular, failed to gather the pace required to usher in modernisation. Nevertheless, due to the fiscal protections accorded to the state, J&K escaped the required central oversight in terms of fund expenditure over the years. This made its audit a challenge for the Central Government.

Nevertheless, the government of India continued to extend cross-sectoral subsidies to the state over the years. For instance, in 1981, the central subsidies directed towards inputs accounted for a substantial Rs 26.03 crores, with additional allocations amounting to Rs 2.65 crores for fertilisers, Rs 20.01

crores for irrigation and Rs 3.38 crores for credit. Furthermore, in tune with the nationwide effort to accelerate the pace of economic growth, a cooperative movement was started. Under this, financial support for crop cultivation and streamlined marketing processes were also extended to J&K. These planned developmental efforts within the agricultural sphere were aligned with the notion of a welfare-maximising 'benevolent state,' as conceptualised by T. N. Srinivasan, and were designed to enhance the standards of living within rural hinterlands.

However, the continued political turmoil since the widely-perceived massively rigged elections in 1987 and recurrent civil unrest that followed it in the region also made it challenging for New Delhi, which remained focused on stabilising the region and addressing its external challenges. This also necessitated a substantial redirection of financial resources, as a significant portion of the funds previously allocated for developmental initiatives had to be diverted towards security expenditure. The heightened security concerns not only hindered the state's economic progress but also posed a formidable challenge to the overall stability of the region.

It is not only the external security expenditure for the state which merits attention, even though this was covered under the defence budget of the Central Government itself. J&K's internal stability also started deteriorating due to the rise in local conflicts and disturbances. This necessitated heightened security measures to maintain law and order, protect civilian lives and curb growing insurgency activities such as those of the Al-Fatah guerrilla group starting from the mid-1970s. The failure of the state government to address such challenges from the outside had devastating consequences in the years ahead, including the diversion of considerable amounts of financial resources, otherwise pledged for developmental projects, towards addressing security concerns. This shift in priorities had notable repercussions on the state's ability to invest in long-term development, impacting infrastructure, education and healthcare initiatives.

However, these challenges aside, the state governments also showed a lackadaisical approach when it came to executing infrastructure projects of extreme socio-economic significance for the region. A CAG report for 1987-88, for instance, reveals that though the J&K government made efforts to undertake the refurbishing of transport connectivity projects through the 'upgrading of the existing roads and construction of new roads...during the successive Plan periods,' the project execution phase faced abnormal delays of between 3 and 26 years. For example, the three State Highway projects of Lehanwan-Patimhal Road, Daksum-Kishtwar Road and Mughal Road, of extreme significance for the intra-regional connectivity in J&K, was not completed even after decades of delay, 'although construction of these roads was taken up as far back as 1976-78, 1971-72 and 1958-59 respectively.'[44]

Likewise, the audit reports are full of half-execution of developmental projects during this period, which resulted in wasted expenditure for the state to the tune of lakhs of rupees every year. This is in addition to the non-maintenance of records by various state government departments for the funds received from the Central Government under special schemes. Take the case of the J&K government's Department of Agriculture: The CAG report of 1984-85 reveals that 'no record of grants released to various implementing agencies during the years 1982-83 to 1984-85 was maintained either by the nodal department (Agriculture Department) or by the two Directorates of Agriculture (Jammu and Kashmir).'[45]

The prevailing political instability and violence in the region created an environment of uncertainty, hindering the progress of developmental activities. The climate of unrest resulted in a slowdown of investments in critical areas such as infrastructure development and other key projects. The reluctance to commit resources to long-term development initiatives was driven by the immediate need to address security challenges and maintain stability. As a consequence, the pace of economic development slowed down significantly, and the state faced limitations in fostering social and economic progress during this turbulent period. These financial allocations were a response to the evolving needs and challenges faced by Jammu and Kashmir during a critical juncture in its history. The prioritisation of security expenditure underscored the imperative of addressing internal conflicts, albeit at the cost of broader developmental efforts. The uncertainty and limited development activities mirrored the complex interplay between political dynamics and economic priorities during this period.

Due to the above reasons, the financial allocations in response to the political turmoil and unrest in J&K during the late 1970s and 1980s played a pivotal role in sustaining the governance in the state and driving its economy. The redirection of funds towards security expenditures and the consequent limitations on developmental initiatives reflected the challenging circumstances faced by the state during this critical phase of its history.

Economic Indicators of J&K and the Role of Central Government

The data accessibility for this period is a real limitation in making micro- and macro-economic trends of the state available. This chapter is, therefore, constrained to rely on select data sets derived from the few available reports of the Comptroller and Auditor General of India (CAG) in this period. It may be noted that the jurisdiction of CAG was extended to the state of J&K only in 1958. While the budgetary documents could not be accessed due to some systematic reasons, the other CAG documents are available for select years on account of 'a fire in the office of the Accountant General, Jammu and Kashmir, Srinagar in March 1977' that destroyed the records related to the state.[46]

The limited data reveals that the state of Jammu and Kashmir remained overtly dependent on central allocations to meet its fiscal demands, as the share of financial proceeds from the government of India remained above 50 per cent throughout. This trend is highlighted in Table 2.2.

Table 2.2 J&K's revenue receipts over the years

Year	Revenue receipts (Rs Cr)	Total central assistance (Rs Cr)	Share of total revenue receipts	Own resources (Rs Cr)	% of total receipts
1977-78	180.3	106.16	59	74.23	41
1978-79	222.88	133.09	60	89.79	40
1980-81	259.3	142.55	55	116.76	45
1981-82	298.58	161.55	54	137.03	46
1982-83	339.48	200.63	59	138.85	41
1984-85	441.67	285.01	65	156.66	35

Data sourced from various CAG reports

J&K ended the fiscal year 1977-78 with a revenue surplus of Rs 39.70 . The total revenue receipts for the said year were recorded at Rs 180.3 , of which an overwhelming 59 per cent (Rs 106.16 crores) constituted grants from the Central Government. This included Rs 14.82 crores as J&K's share of proceeds in the centrally collected taxes, Rs 42.23 crores as statutory grants, Rs

36.34 crores as block grants for State Plan schemes, Rs 4.52 crores as grants for Central Plan schemes and Rs 4.01 crores as grants for Centrally Sponsored Plan schemes, along with Rs 4.24 crores under Non-Plan grants (other than those included in statutory grants). At the same time, it may be noted that J&K raised tax and non-tax resources worth Rs 74.23 during this period, which constituted 41 per cent of the state's total revenue resources for the fiscal year 1977-78 (see Figure 2.1).

Figure 2.1 Trend of central assistance to J&K

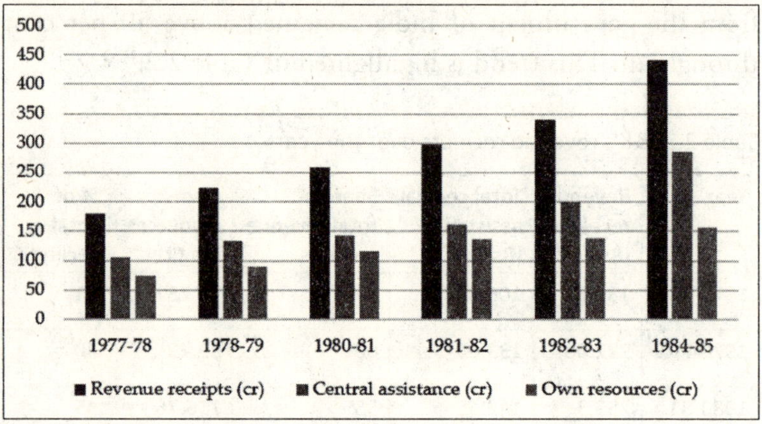

Date sourced from the different CAG reports on J&K

Further, the Central Government extended loans and advances worth Rs 80.22 crores during this period, which increased J&K's outstanding amounts towards the Central Government to Rs 597.63 , constituting 96 per cent of the state's total public debt, by the end of March 1979. By the end of March 1988, J&K's total debt liability jumped to Rs 2,310.25 , which included Rs 1,728.98 crores in loans and advances from the Central Government. These loans constituted nearly 75 per cent of J&K's public debts.

Towards the end of the 1980s, J&K went on a downward spiral with the breakdown of the law-and-order situation, which also pushed the government machinery out of order, with development taking a back seat and restoration of order taking precedence. The macro-economic figures of the erstwhile state reflect these exigencies. For instance, from an amount of Rs 285.01 crores as Central Assistance for J&K in 1984-85, this figure declined to Rs 56.13 crores by 1986-87, thereby demonstrating a staggering decrease of 80.31 per cent. This decreased further to Rs 50.72 crores by 1987-88 before experiencing a gradual trend reversal by 1988-89, when it increased to Rs 122.24 crores (see Figure 2.2).

Figure 2.2 Trend of central assistance to J&K

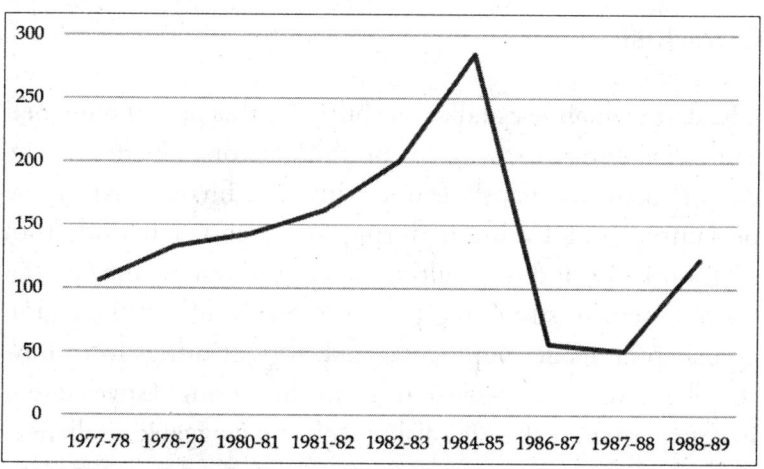

Data sourced from CAG reports on J&K

The CAG Report for J&K in 1988-89 castigated the state government of Dr Farooq Abdullah for having failed to expand the industrial base in the region. It noted that while the Central Government recognised J&K as an industrially backward state to ensure that the local government receives affirmative treatment with added funds, it had failed to make any turnaround in the situation. 'No serious efforts have been made to industrialise the 'No Industry Districts' and other less affluent areas, and about 78 per cent of Central Investment Subsidy (CIS) was spent on Jammu, Srinagar and Budgam districts alone. No. growth centres have been developed away from the existing industrial centres,' the CAG report noted.[47] It further noted that there was a lack of coordination between various government departments. For instance, in the period '1986-87 to 1988-89, only 36 per cent of cases recommended by the District Industries Centres could get assistance from the financial institutions. Delays in payment of subsidy to the entrepreneurs in almost 50 per cent of the cases reviewed in audit exceeded one year.'

Conclusion

The data availability and accessibility for this period remained somewhat limited owing to multiple factors. Therefore, the chapter provides snapshots of the intricate financial landscape of Jammu and Kashmir, during an extended period from 1947 to 1989, and the multifaceted role played by the Central Government in sustaining the economic health of the region and shaping its developmental trajectory. It brings forth how the liberal financial provisions from the Central Government have proved pivotal in stabilising J&K as it navigated challenges from the Pakistani and also Chinese aggression on its borders.

The 1950s marked a shift towards long-term economic development and modernisation, empowered by the unique autonomous status granted to the state under Article 370. In contrast, the 1960s witnessed efforts of the Central Government to expand the economic base of the state by making allocations for refurbishing the infrastructural requirements of the topographically challenged region to usher in development. Serious efforts were also made to strengthen the tourism industry in the region, which has over the years emerged as a significant sector of J&K's economy.

The perpetual challenges that the state faced since 1947 need to be recognised. However, these provide no explanation or justification for the pervasive developmental deficit and the severe gaps in delivering governance on the part of the state government. The macroeconomic indicators of J&K indicate that the state has exhibited an entrenched reliance on central resources, with the state government failing to expand the industrial base despite receiving regular incentives and subsidies from the Central Government towards that end.

Chapter III

Advent of Sponsored Militancy (1989-1998)
The Forced Backslide

THE LATE 1980s marked the beginning of a tumultuous period in the history of Jammu and Kashmir (J&K), characterised by the commencement of a Pakistan-sponsored armed insurgency. This insurgency hastened J&K's catastrophic descent into chaos and anarchy, as the law and order machinery suffered a significant setback because of the scale of violence perpetuated by these groups. The protracted violence and insurgency created an environment of insecurity and instability, which resulted in disruptions in the normal life of the state and took a heavy toll on every aspect of the people's lives as the social, political, and economic landscape of J&K was profoundly impacted and altered, with far-reaching consequences. The region is yet to emerge from the ramifications of this period, which serve as a reminder of the multifaceted challenges and tribulations it and its people have continued to face.

In the late 1980s, J&K had an elected National Conference (NC)–Congress alliance government led by the Chief Minister, Farooq Abdullah. However, starting from 1987, the mounting insurgency, along with the political turbulence it caused, worsened the law and order situation in the region. Additionally, Abdullah had strong disagreement with the VP Singh-led Central Government in New Delhi on various issues, particularly on the imminent reappointment of Jagmohan Malhotra as the Governor of J&K in early 1990. It is notable to remember that Jagmohan, during his first stint as Governor of J&K (26 April 1984—11 July 1989), had dismissed Farooq Abdulah's government in 1984. A day before Jagmohan's assumption of office on 19 January 1990, Farooq Abdullah resigned from chief ministership protesting the move. This led to the fall of the NC—Congress government. NC called Jagmohan's appointment and the consequent departure of Abdullah's elected government a blatant blow to democracy. The J&K Legislative Assembly was put on suspended animation and dissolved a month later on 19 February 1990, thereby bringing in Governor's Rule for an initial period of six months. In May 1990, Jagmohan was replaced by Girish Chandra Saxena, a career police officer and former head of Research and Analysis Wing (RAW). The expiry of Governor's Rule plunged J&K into an extended period of President's Rule, which lasted for 6 years and 264 days—from 18 July 1990 till 9 October 1996. This gave the Central Government full administrative control of the state government machinery, thereby allowing it to take a more direct role in implementing measures to combat militancy.

It took concerted efforts from the Central Government and state security machinery to contain the violence unleashed by the militant groups and bring a semblance of normalcy to the region, enabling efforts to hold elections by September–October 1996. The government of India headed by the then Prime Minister H. D. Deve Gowda, who promised 'maximum autonomy' for the region, succeeded in holding the elections to the state assembly. This saw the participation of the National Conference (NC), which had earlier boycotted the Lok Sabha General Election of 1996. NC won an overwhelming mandate by winning 57 (almost two-thirds) of the 87 seats and formed the government with Farooq Abdullah as the chief minister. He continued his tenure until the next elections in 2002. The People's Democratic Party (PDP) emerged as a new party with a base in the valley (16 seats compared to 28 seats won by NC) in the elections of 2002 under the leadership of Mufti Mohammad Sayeed, and formed the government in alliance with the Congress (20 seats). Ever since the successful conduct of the 1996 elections, there was a marked transition to democratic governance in the state, and this was seen as a mandate against secessionist forces, who had been weakened by the government's efforts by then.

Notwithstanding this, Pakistan-sponsored militancy and insurgency ravaged the economic sphere of the state. It caused a significant loss of human capital; casualties grew from the violence perpetuated by these groups, which exacerbated the 'brain drain,' as educated youth and skilled professionals were forced to leave in search of safer and more stable environments. Moreover, the 1990s also witnessed a near-total uprooting of the Kashmiri Hindu community (called Pandits in local parlance). Nearly 90,000—100,000 out of the population of Pandits—about 140,000—left the valley.[48] The region is yet to recover from the outmigration of talent, with the economy deprived of the skilled human resources necessary for growth and diversification.

The large-scale insurgency exacted a heavy toll on public infrastructure, particularly critical communication structures such as road networks, bridges, and culverts. The repercussions were staggering, resulting in extensive damage to the vital infrastructure of the state. The 1995-96 report of the Ministry of Home Affairs (MHA), Government of India reveals that a total of 338 bridges and culverts, 1,219 government buildings, 1,178 shops, 702 educational institutions, 8,612 privately-owned properties, and 7 hospitals were destroyed in over 4,127 instances of militant and subversive acts from 1988 to March 1996.[49] This relentless assault on infrastructure had profound socio-economic implications, as it disrupted not only the flow of goods, services, and daily life but also engendered a pervasive atmosphere of uncertainty and instability, thereby further exacerbating the multifaceted challenges faced by the populace.

One of the most apparent economic casualties of insurgency in J&K was the tourism sector. With its breathtaking natural beauty, cultural diversity and historical heritage, the region was a popular tourist destination, especially among foreigners, mostly Europeans. The insurgency led to negative press coverage and deterred tourists from visiting the area. The constant threat of violence, including terrorist attacks and insurgency-related incidents, coupled with frequent curfews and heightened security concerns, made travellers apprehensive about their safety. This was exacerbated by incidents like the infamous kidnapping of six western tourist hikers in July 1995 from Liddarwat, Pahalgam in Anantnag district by the Al-Faran militant group, an offshoot of Harkat-ul Ansar, to secure release of Masood Azhar, who was then in the custody of Indian police due to his role in organizing militancy in Kashmir. This followed the unsuccessful kidnapping earlier in September-October 1994 for the same purpose. The 1995 kidnapping was infamous because one of the hostages, Hans Christian Ostro, was beheaded by militants six weeks later. One of these, an American, managed to escape, while nothing is known about the rest of the four hostages till today. Following this, there was a sharp decline in tourist arrivals, causing a substantial loss of revenue for the tourism industry.

A Ministry of Home Affairs Report of 2004-05 noted that while tourism sector possessed a significant potential for driving J&K's economic growth and generating employment, it was 'one of the worst-hit sectors during the turmoil in Jammu & Kashmir in the early 1990s' when 'a large part tourism-related infrastructure got damaged'. This brought down the tourist arrival to 'an all-time low in 1995.'[50] The decline in tourist footfall resulted in economic losses for a wide range of businesses associated with the tourism sector, including hotels, restaurants, tour operators and handicraft markets. Further, as this sector provided livelihood to a large number of people in the region, the violence directly impacted the tour guides, hotel staff and other individuals engaged in various tourism-related activities.

Likewise, other sectors of the economy were also impacted, and this decline in economic activity exacerbated the economic downturn of the region. This chapter provides a comprehensive overview of the budgetary allocations made by the government from 1989-90 to 1997-98, during which time J&K remained mostly under President's Rule.

To end this economic stagnancy and development, the Central Government initiated measures to reinvigorate and expedite the pace of economic development in the state, with particular emphasis on the Kashmir valley. This strategy encompassed an increase in Central plan assistance to bridge the non-plan resource deficit and the vigilant oversight of plan execution at all levels, aimed at ensuring the efficient utilisation of available resources without any wastage. Numerous high-level teams of Central officials were constituted to closely monitor the progression of developmental activities within the state while engaging in comprehensive interactions with the state authorities.

Simultaneously, the Central Government established the Department for Jammu & Kashmir Affairs in 1994 to evaluate the state's challenges and facilitate the normalisation of the development process. The concerted efforts undertaken at the Central level were complemented by a revitalised commitment from the state Government to enhance the efficiency of its administrative apparatus, particularly at the grassroots level. The government made special efforts to revive and accelerate the pace of economic development in the state, particularly in the Kashmir valley. The strategy comprised enhanced Central plan assistance to meet the non-plan resource gap and intensive monitoring of plan implementation at all levels to ensure that the available resources were utilised gainfully without leakage. Several high-level Central teams of officials constituted for closely monitoring developmental activities visited the state for wide-ranging interactions with the state authorities.[51]

Overview of J&K's Financial Health in the 1989-98

The financial health of J&K, as lawlessness broke down the state machinery, was very poor, with a debt of Rs 2724.04 crores, which was more than three times its revenue receipts. The fiscal year of 1987-88 had seen state accounts close with a revenue deficit of Rs 71.76 crore, which increased to Rs 92.94 crore. J&K received Rs 122.24 crores in grants-in-aid for Central and Centrally Sponsored Plan Schemes from the Central Government, significantly increasing from Rs 50.72 crores in the previous financial year.

With the Governor's Rule in place, followed by an extended period of President's Rule, the state machinery effectively came under the direct control of the Central Government in Delhi, with most of its administrative affairs managed by the Ministry of Home Affairs. For the 1990-91 fiscal year, parliament approved a Supplementary Demand of Grants of Rs 11.57 crores in Revenue and Rs 9.06 crores in Capital accounts to the budgetary allocations of the state to account for the exceeded expenditure through the Jammu and Kashmir Appropriation (Vote on Account) Bill 2, 1991, on 11 March 1991.

During the President's Rule spanning 1990-96, the Union Finance Ministry presented the annual budget of J&K in the Parliament of India. In the annual budget for the 1991-92 fiscal year, the Union Government allocated Rs 661.5 crores and Rs 437.8 crores in Revenue and Capital Accounts, respectively. It further approved Rs 43.30 crores and Rs 10.74 crores in Revenue and Capital resources through the Supplementary Demand of Grants for the year to take care of the exceeded expenditure of the state administration. Table 3.1 shows the yearly budgetary allocations under the Revenue and Capital heads.

Table 3.1 Annual budget allocations during 1990-97

Year	Revenue (crore)	Capital (crore)
1991-92	661.5	437.8
1992-93	645.4	457.1
1993-94	795.0	510.2
1994-95	951.7	546.1
1995-96	1114.8	700.4
1996-97	1342.8	682.2
CAGR	12.52 per cent	7.67 per cent

Source: CAG Reports for J&K, Budget documents as available in the digital library of the Parliament of India.

As the data demonstrates, the fiscal allocations of the state witnessed marginal growth over these years, with a Compound Annual Growth Rate (CAGR) of 12.53 per cent and 7.67 per cent in revenue and capital allocations respectively (see Figure 3.1).

Figure 3.1 Annual revenue and capital allocations

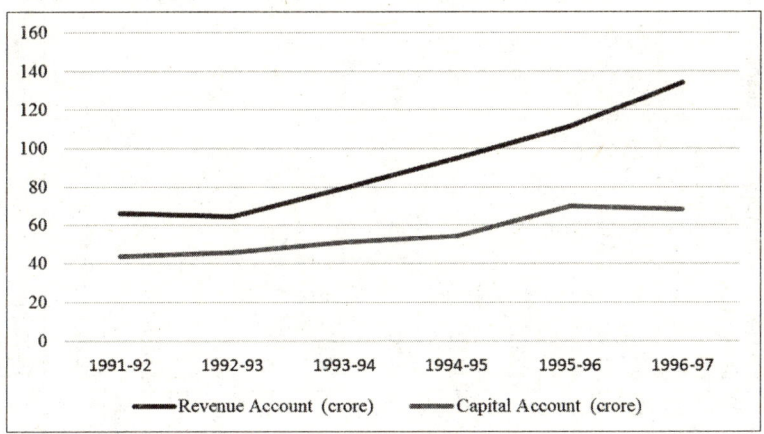

Source: CAG Reports

In terms of the Central Government's assistance to J&K during this period, it has remained a primary source of revenue for the state. As can be observed in Table 3.2, the share of the Union Government through grants-in-aid and central taxes remained on an average of over 80 per cent during the 1988-1998 period. The grants-in-aid from the Central Government witnessed a CAGR of 20.64 per cent, shown in the figure below, whereas J&K's Central Tax Share grew at a CAGR of 16.77 per cent.

The share of grants-in-aid in J&K's Revenue Receipts is shown in Figure 3.2. During the 1988-89 fiscal year, J&K received central assistance of Rs 666 crore. It included Rs176.75 crore as the state's share in the Central taxes and grants-in-aid in Plan and Non-Plan Grants for Central and Centrally Sponsored Schemes.[52] The CAG Report for 1988-89 further stated that J&K Government's total debt liability stood at Rs 2,724.04 crores, including loans and advances amounting to Rs 2,039.04 crores from the Government of India.

Table 3.2 J&K's revenue receipts during the 1988-98 period

Year	Revenue receipts	Increase (+) / decrease (-) over the previous year	Grants-in-aid (Cr)	Per cent of total receipts	state's central tax share (Cr)	Per cent of total receipts	Total central assistance (Cr)	Share of total Central Resources	Own resources	Per cent of total receipts
1988-89	927	(+) 23	489	53	177	19	666	72	261	28
1989-90	960	(+) 4	478	50	233	24	711	74	249	26
1990-91	1535	(+) 60	907	59	376	25	1283	84	252	16
1991-92	1717	(+) 12	1032	60	410	24	1442	84	275	16
1992-93	2027	(+) 18	1200	59	480	24	1680	83	347	17
1993-94	2179	(+) 8	1300	60	510	23	1810	83	369	17
1994-95	3088	(+) 42	2126	69	563	18	2689	87	399	13
1995-96	3319	(+) 7	2179	66	644	19	2823	85	496	15
1996-97	3223	(-) 3	2120	66	626	19	2746	85	477	15
1997-98	4642	(+) 44	3192	69	834	18	4026	87	616	13
CAGR	17.48 per cent		20.64 per cent		16.77 per cent		19.71 per cent		8.97 per cent	

Figure 3.2 Grants-in-aid in J&K's revenue receipts

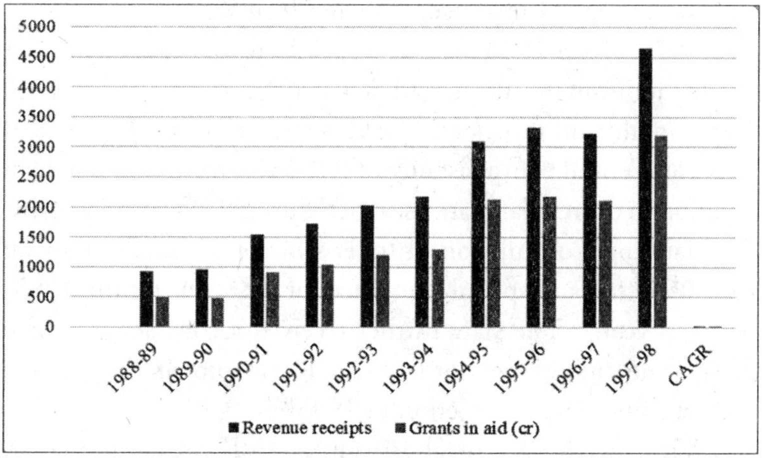

Source: CAG Reports

In the budget estimates for the fiscal year 1989-90, the J&K government had estimated a revenue surplus of Rs 5 crores. However, the state, in actuality, in line with the trend since 1986-87, recorded a revenue deficit of Rs 136 crores. J&K's Audit report for 1989-90 highlighted that the state's liabilities grew by 94 per cent in this period, going from Rs 1,733.88 crores to Rs 3,362.71 crores. The only positive for the state was its concurrent increase in assets by 67 per cent, rising from Rs 1,969.72 crores to Rs 3288.21 crores during this period.[53]

The available data reveals that the J&K Government's revenue receipts saw a 60 per cent rise from Rs 600.51 crores in 1985-86 to Rs 960.00 crores in 1989-90. The combined sum received by the state, comprising the state's share of Central Tax proceeds and grants-in-aid, increased from Rs 404.56 crores to Rs 711.13 crores between 1985-86 and 1989-90, thereby marking a 76 per cent increase. As seen in Table, the grants-in-aid to J&K witnessed a record increase in two instances in the 1988-98 period. First, it jumped from Rs 1,300 crores in 1993-94 to Rs 2,126 crores in 1994-95, and in the second instance, it soared from Rs 2,120 crores in 1996-97 to Rs 3,192 crores in 1997-98 fiscal year.

In addition to the scheduled central assistance, such as grants-in-aid and tax shares, the Government of India provided 'a special Central plan assistance of Rs 973 crores... to the state in addition to the regular plan assistance' during 1994-95. Similarly, the Planning Commission of India sanctioned an allocation of Rs 1,053 crores as special assistance for J&K during the 1995-96 fiscal year.[54] The state further received a considerable share of funding under the Border Area Development Programme (BADP) since its introduction in 1993-94.

With increased central assistance, J&K's revenue deficit, estimated in the annual budget of 1990-91 at Rs 91 crores, changed into a revenue surplus of Rs 287 crores in the fiscal year. This transformation majorly happened because of an exponential increase in the grants-in-aid to the state from the preceding year's Rs 478 crores to Rs 907 crores.[55] The state's financial accounts continued to show a revenue surplus in its accounts during this period. A tabulated trend of revenue surplus/deficit is shown in Table 3.3, while the graphical trend is captured in Figure 3.3.

Table 3.3 Trend of J&K's revenue account

Year	Revenue Surplus (crores)
1988-89	(-) 93
1989-90	(-) 136
1990-91	287
1991-92	64
1992-93	215
1993-94	58
1994-95	562
1995-96	505
1996-97	94
1997-98	451

Source: CAG Annual Reports

Figure 3.3 Revenue surplus (crores)

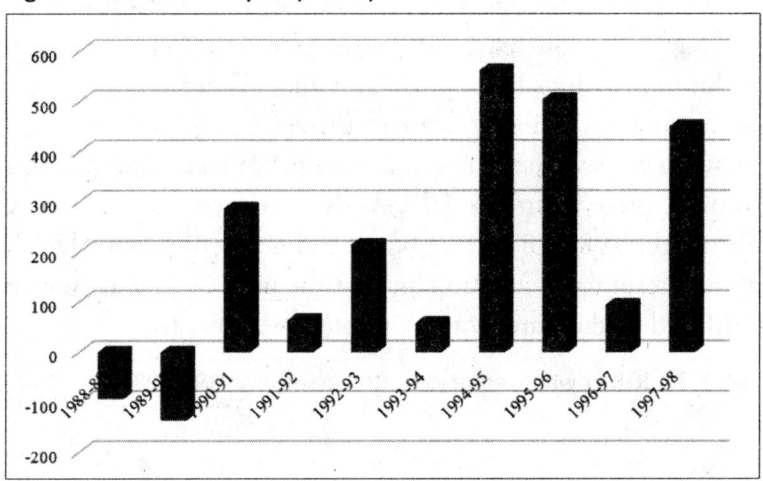

Source: CAG Annual Reports

Figure 3.4 Central assistance against J&K's revenue receipts

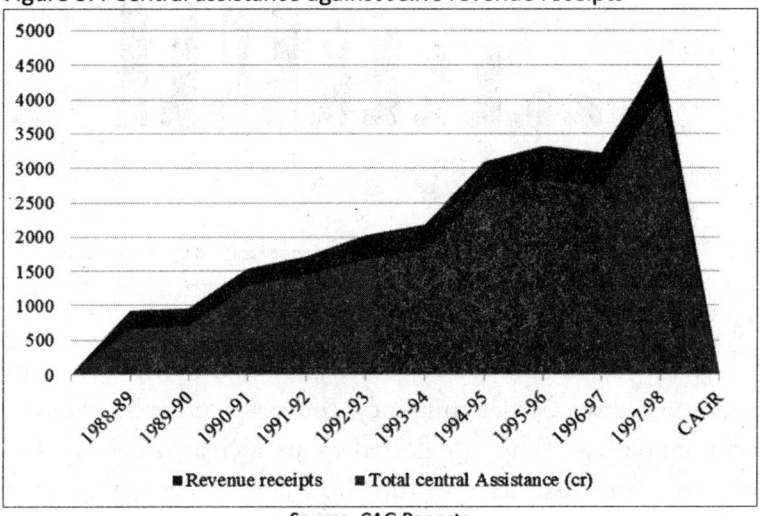

Source: CAG Reports

When grants-in-aid from the Central Government are taken together with J&K's share in Union tax collection, it can be seen that the total Central Assistance to the state, as is shown in Figure 3.4, grew at a CAGR of 19.71 per cent during this period.

Despite the central assistance, J&K could not streamline its revenue collection system, which is reflected in its generation of limited financial resources and high dependence on the government of India for its expenditure. As is shown in figure, J&K's own revenue generation, from both tax and non-tax sources, grew at an annual CAGR of a mere 8.97 per cent during the 1988-98 period. Figure 3.5 below highlights J&K's annual resource generation against the total central assistance delivered to the state by the Union Government.

Figure 3.5 J&K's own revenue vs central assistance (1988-98)

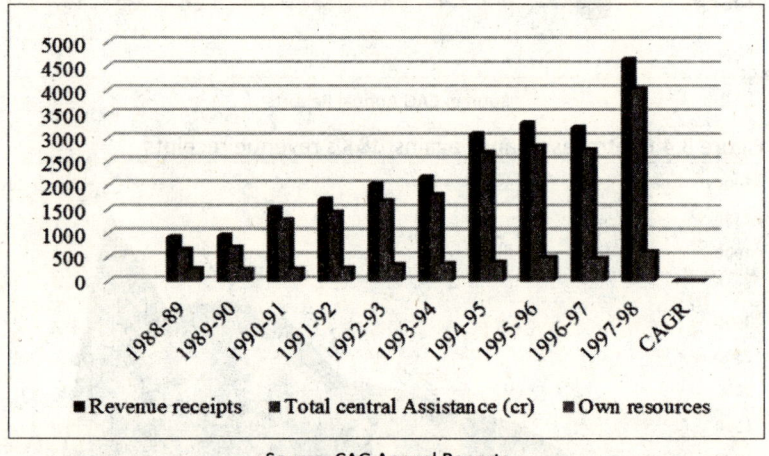

Source: CAG Annual Reports

With J&K's governance severely affected by the Pakistan-sponsored cross-border militancy, the state entered a sluggish economic phase. This is reflected by its increased dependence on the central assistance to run the affairs of the state. Figure 3.6 shows the changed dynamics of the state's Revenue sources. J&K's own revenue generation as a percentage of its total Revenue Receipts, which was recorded at 28 per cent in 1988-89, saw a sharp decline with the uptick in militancy to 16 per cent in 1990-91. By the end of the fiscal year 1997-98, the state was back in the democratic fold, following the successful 1996 election bringing Farooq Abdullah-led National Conference to power. However, J&K's extreme dependence on central assistance further aggravated, with its local resource generation recorded as a mere 13 per cent of its total Revenue Receipts.

Figure 3.6 Central assistance vs J&K's own resources as percentage of J&K's total revenue receipts

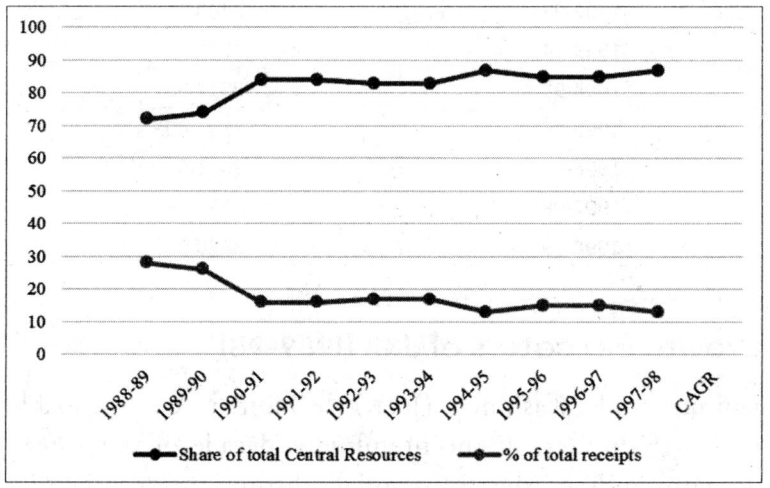

Source: CAG Annual Reports

Besides these allocations in the form of grants-in-aid share in central taxes, the Government of India provided the state government with substantial financial capital as loans and advances to help alleviate the J&K government's financial constraints as the local resource generation receded. Table 3.4 shows the loans and advances from the Central Government during the 1988-98 period.

Further, the Ministry of Home Affairs allocated a substantial sum of money during this period to refurbish the security-related infrastructure of J&K. For instance, during the 1995-96 fiscal year, J&K received Rs 81,540 lakhs under the police modernisation scheme from MHA. J&K remains one of the primary beneficiaries of this scheme.

Table 3.4 Loans and advances from the Central Government

Year	Amount (crores)
1988-89	1728.98
1989-90	2039.04
1990-91	2412.42
1991-92	2422.09
1992-93	2400.97
1993-94	2511.52
1994-95	2517.58
1995-96	2584.40
1996-97	3028.61
1997-98	3231.08
1998-99	3420.18

Source: CAG Reports

Growth Indicators of J&K (1989-98)

Jammu and Kashmir (J&K) exhibited commendable resilience throughout the tumultuous decade of the 1990s, notwithstanding the substantial disruptions caused by widespread violence of Pakistan-sponsored militant groups, which left an indelible impact on the state's economic landscape. One of the pivotal metrics for gauging the overarching economic performance and productivity of a given region is the Net State Domestic Product (NSDP). This metric, encapsulating the monetary value of all goods and services generated within a state or locality over a specified temporal horizon, reveals a noteworthy Compound Annual Growth Rate (CAGR) of 16.67 per cent during the period spanning from 1990 to 1999.

J&K started the tumultuous decade with the NSDP at current price levels of Rs 2,908 crore, steadily increasing to Rs 11,128 crore by the end of the 1998-99 fiscal year. This upward trajectory is emblematic of its resilience despite its formidable challenges from the cross-border inimical forces. The annual growth trend of NSDP at current prices is shown in Figure 3.7.

Figure 3.7 Trend of J&K's NSDP at current prices during 1990-99 period

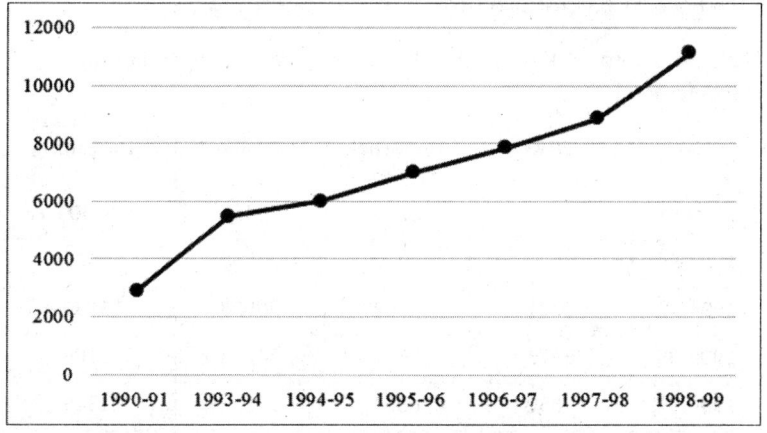

Source: Indiabudget.gov.in

A comparative analysis between Jammu and Kashmir (J&K) and its neighbouring North Indian states, namely Himachal Pradesh, Haryana and Punjab, makes it evident that the Compound Annual Growth Rate (CAGR) of J&K's Net State Domestic Product (NSDP) at current prices stood at a noteworthy 16.74 per cent during the specified period, ranking second in performance. Only Haryana surpassed this achievement with a remarkable CAGR of 22.01 per cent. Following J&K, Himachal Pradesh and Punjab exhibited substantial CAGR figures of 14.57 per cent and 13.04 per cent respectively. It is imperative, however, to underscore that these CAGR values do not equate to the actual NSDP figures themselves. They represent the annualised growth rates over the specified period, elucidating the dynamic nature of economic development within these regions. The precise NSDP figures provide a more concrete and nuanced perspective on the economic scale and productivity of each state. As is evident from Table 3.5 and Figure 3.8, Punjab's NSDP at current prices increased from Rs 16,542 crores in 1990-91 to Rs 49,588 crores in 1998-99. Similarly, Haryana's NSDP at current prices jumped from Rs 6,390 crores in 1990-91 to Rs 38,288 crores in 1998-99.

Table 3.5 Jammu & Kashmir NSDP at current rates vs neighbouring states (crores)

Year	J&K	Himachal Pradesh	Punjab	Haryana
1990-91	2908	2795	16452	6390
1993-94	5500	4250	27068	19422
1994-95	6001	5192	30528	23136
1995-96	6973	5930	34218	26166
1996-97	7851	6803	39112	31345
1997-98	8858	7807	43096	33910
1998-99	11128	9507	49588	38288
CAGR	16.74 per cent	14.57 per cent	13.04 per cent	22.01 per cent

Source: Indiabudget.gov.in

Figure 3.8 NSDP of J&K vs HP, Punjab & Haryana at current prices (in crores)

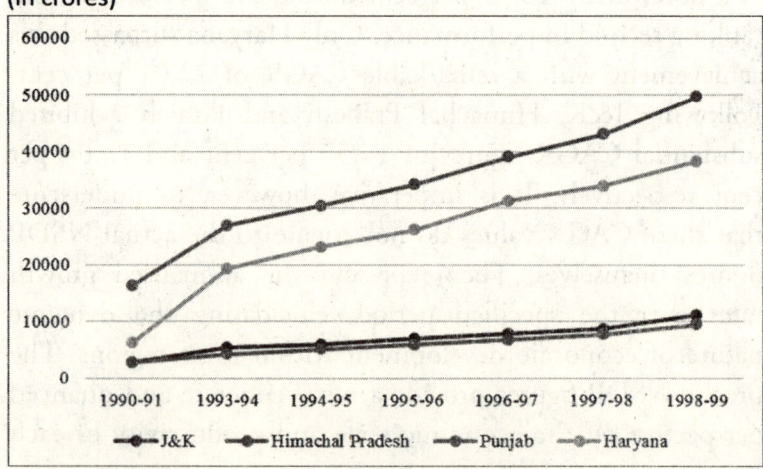

Source: Indiabudget.gov.in

In terms of per capita NSDP at current prices, Jammu and Kashmir (J&K) commenced the 1990s with Rs 3,816 in the fiscal year 1990-91, which then surged to Rs 11,591 by the fiscal year 1998-99, indicating a Compound Annual Growth Rate (CAGR) of 13.14 per cent throughout this period (see Figure 3.9).

Figure 3.9 J&K's per capita NSDP at current prices against neighbouring states

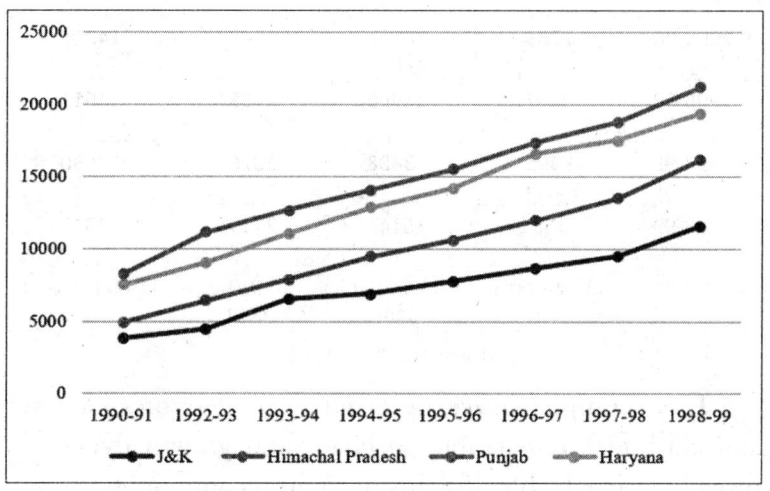

Source: Indiabudget.gov.in

Despite having a significantly lower population, the smaller state of Himachal Pradesh exhibited a more robust CAGR of 14.14 per cent. It increased from Rs 4,910 during the 1990-91 fiscal year to Rs 16,144 by 1998-99, which is 28 per cent higher compared to J&K. In contrast, even though the neighbouring states of Punjab and Haryana displayed lower CAGR figures than J&K, as depicted in Table 3.6, their per capita NSDP of Rs 21,195 and Rs 19,340 would surpass J&K's by 45 per cent and 40 per cent respectively.

Table 3.6 Per Capita NSDP at current prices (in Rs)

Year	J&K	Himachal Pradesh	Punjab	Haryana
1990-91	3816	4910	8318	7508
1992-93	4457	6390	11140	9037
1993-94	6543	7870	12710	11079
1994-95	6915	9451	14066	12879
1995-96	7783	10607	15471	14213
1996-97	8667	11960	17353	16611
1997-98	9491	13488	18764	17530
1998-99	11591	16144	21195	19340
CAGR	13.14 per cent	14.14 per cent	10.95 per cent	11.09 per cent

Source: Indiabudget.gov.in

This comprehensive assessment underscores Jammu and Kashmir's remarkable resilience and growth dynamics, providing invaluable insights into its economic trajectory amid challenging circumstances and regional comparisons. However, the infusion of large assistance by the successive governments in New Delhi played an important role in helping J&K navigate this disruptive phase.

Conclusion

The late 1980s marked the inception of a tumultuous and harrowing era in the history of Jammu and Kashmir (J&K). The Pakistan-sponsored armed insurgency plunged the region into a state of chaos and anarchy, leaving an enduring imprint on every facet of life within the state. The violence and instability generated by the insurgency had profound and far-reaching consequences, manifesting across the social, political and economic landscape.

Despite the presence of an elected government during the initial stages of this period, the mounting militancy insurgency posed formidable challenges to governance and law enforcement. It was only through concerted efforts and the commitment of the central and state administrations led by the Governor, alongside security measures, that some semblance of normalcy was gradually restored to the region. The successful conduct of elections in 1996 marked a significant turning point, indicating the waning influence of secessionist forces and a transition to democratic governance.

However, the economic toll exacted by the insurgency was substantial. Infrastructure, critical for economic progress, bore the brunt of the violence, leading to extensive damage and disruption. Once a thriving economic driver, the tourism sector suffered significant setbacks due to security concerns and negative perceptions. This decline had a cascading effect on various businesses and livelihoods associated with the industry.

To counter this economic stagnation and drive development, the Central Government initiated measures to bolster the region's economy, particularly in the Kashmir valley. Enhanced central plan assistance, rigorous plan implementation oversight, and high-level monitoring teams were deployed to ensure efficient resource utilisation.

The financial health of J&K during this period reflected its heavy reliance on central assistance. While the state's revenue generation lagged, central assistance played a pivotal role in sustaining its financial stability. The share of grants-in-aid and central taxes remained substantial throughout this period, contributing significantly to the state's revenue.

Economic growth indicators, particularly the Net State Domestic Product (NSDP), underscored the region's resilience. Despite the tumultuous decade, J&K exhibited a semblance of growth. Comparative analysis with neighbouring states highlighted J&K's economic performance, revealing a better growth trajectory but also emphasising the need for further development and diversification even as it battled insurgency.

Therefore, Jammu and Kashmir's journey through the 1990s was marked by profound challenges and tribulations, particularly in the economic sphere. While it demonstrated resilience and growth, the scars of the insurgency continued to influence the region's trajectory, emphasising the imperative of sustained efforts to restore and diversify its economy.

Chapter IV

Revival of Democratic Governance and The Developmental Lag (1998-2019)

THE 1990S marked a tumultuous decade for Jammu & Kashmir (J&K) and its residents, defined by pervasive violence orchestrated by Pakistan-backed factions. A significant turning point emerged in 1996, when the state conducted elections for its legislative Assembly, signifying a major democratic milestone. During this election, the J&K National Conference secured a resounding victory, capturing 57 out of 87 seats in the Assembly. Subsequent to the successful electoral process, the Government of India embarked on a determined path to quell Pakistan's proxy violence and intensify developmental initiatives for the region.

The economic trajectory of the former state of Jammu and Kashmir between 1998 and 2019 presented a complex interplay of factors that have significantly influenced its financial landscape. This period was marked by distinctive trends, with the state receiving a disproportionately high share of central grants, prompting a deep examination of its economic dynamics. A pivotal report by the Comptroller and Auditor General (CAG) in 2016 shed light on the state's exceptional reliance on central funds, revealing stark discrepancies in grant distribution compared to other major states such as Uttar Pradesh.[56] This report delves into the economic situation of

Jammu and Kashmir during the specified period, emphasising its financial dependency, resource allocation, and implications for sustainable development.

From 1998 to 2019, J&K stood out by receiving a substantially higher proportion of central grants in comparison to all other states in India. The CAG report 2016 disclosed a striking statistic J&K accounted for 10 per cent of all Central grants disbursed to states between 2000 and 2016. In contrast, the state of Uttar Pradesh, which accounted for 13 per cent of the total population of the country, received only 8.2 per cent of Central grants during the same timeframe. Remarkably, this figure is particularly astonishing considering that the state's population constituted a mere one per cent of the entire country's population. Such disproportionate allocation of central grants underscores a unique financial arrangement that shaped J&K's economic landscape during this timeframe, and it highlights the exceptional nature of J&K's financial relationship with the Central Government. Notably, the substantial difference in the percentage of grants further accentuates the economic challenges and imperatives that characterised J&K's financial governance.[57]

The population-adjusted grant allocation unveils the unique nature of central grants received by Jammu and Kashmir. With a population of 12.55 million (as per the 2011 Census) J&K obtained an average of Rs 91,300 per person over the sixteen-year period under consideration in the CAG report. In contrast, Uttar Pradesh, with a population of unparalleled size (199.8 million in 2011), received merely Rs 4,300 per person over the same period. This per capita analysis starkly demonstrates the distinct pattern of resource allocation, indicating J&K's higher reliance on external financial support.[58]

The exceptional allocation of grants, juxtaposed with

allocation for Uttar Pradesh, the state with the largest population in India, illustrates a significant financial imbalance that underscores the broader challenges of fiscal autonomy and sustainable development. The unique grant distribution model, which saw J&K receiving a substantially higher proportion of central funds despite its population size, raises pertinent questions about resource management, governance and long-term economic sustainability. As the region navigated a complex socio-political environment, these economic dynamics shed light on the intricate interplay between external support and internal financial management. The report's findings emphasise the need for strategic resource generation, fiscal prudence and policy measures to ensure Jammu and Kashmir's sustained development in the face of evolving political and economic landscapes.

Despite this liberal financial funding received by the J&K Government, it failed to improve its economic indicators. The publicly available data collected from budget documents, economic surveys and CAG reports reveal that J&K lagged behind its neighbouring states such as Himachal Pradesh by significant margins in the economic indicators. For instance, the Economic Survey 2016 highlighted significant disparities between J&K and Himachal Pradesh (HP) despite its larger population and geographical area. The survey revealed that the Gross State Domestic Product (GSDP)[59] of J&K, with its net area of 1,01,387 square kilometres and a population of 1.25 crores, for 2015-16 was Rs 91,806 crore, and per capita income stood at Rs 57,858, with a growth rate of 7.79% over the previous year. In comparison, Himachal Pradesh, with a smaller area of 55,673 square kilometres and a population of 6.8 million, exhibited a higher GSDP of Rs 95,929 crores and per capita income of Rs 1,11,977, with a growth rate of 7.72%. Specifically, J&K's GSDP, Net State Domestic

Product (NSDP)[60], and per capita NSDP are lower than HP by significant margins: GSDP (Constant) less by Rs 4,123 crores (2015-16), NSDP (Constant) less by Rs 2,263 crores (2015-16), and per capita NSDP (Constant 2015-16) less by Rs 54,119.[61]

A broader comparison of J&K with its neighbouring states during the 2014-2019 period is highlighted in Tables 4.1 (showing GSDP figures) and 4.2 (showing per capita NSDP figures). Though the state had a better Cumulative Aggregate Growth Rate (CAGR) of 5.7, it had failed to expand the volume of its economy.

Table 4.1 Comparison of GSDP of J&K with GSDP of neighbouring states (in crores)

Year	All India	J&K	Punjab	Delhi	HP	Haryana	UP
2014-15	10527674	82372	312125	428355	89060	370535	834432
2015-16	11369493	97001	330052	475623	96274	413405	908241
2016-17	12308193	100199	352721	511765	103055	456709	1011500
2017-18	13144582	106624	375406	542015	109406	482036	1056399
2018-19	13992914	115062	397019	565327	116411	524171	1097353
CAGR	7.37	8.71	6.20	7.18	6.92	9.06	7.09

Source: Economic Survey 2023

Table 4.2 Comparison of per capita income (per capita NSDP at current prices) of J&K with those of neighbouring states

Year	J&K	Punjab	Delhi	HP	Haryana	UP
2014-15	62327	108970	247209	123299	147382	42267
2015-16	74950	118858	270261	135512	164963	47118
2016-17	78960	128780	295558	150290	184982	52671
2017-18	87710	139835	318323	165497	208437	57944
2018-19	98738	149974	338730	174804	223015	62350
CAGR	12.19	8.31	8.19	9.12	10.91	10.21

Source: Economic Survey 2023

Despite having only 55% of the geographical area and population compared to J&K, Himachal Pradesh's GSDP at constant prices is 4.30% higher than J&K's. While both states experienced growth in 2015-16, HP's growth rate of 7.72% has been consistent. In contrast, J&K's growth rate has varied over the past four years.

Tourism, a crucial industry for both states, presents a notable contrast. J&K's tourist inflow for 2015 was 92.03 lakh tourists, lower than HP's 175.31 lakh tourists, despite J&K's scenic beauty and attractions. Additionally, hydel power potential is estimated at 20,000 MWs for both states, but HP has harnessed 32% of its potential, while J&K only exploited 16%.

Furthermore, J&K lags behind HP in terms of industries, with fewer large and medium-scale industries and lower employment figures. J&K's net area sown is only 7% of the total area, compared to HP's 12%. The survey attributes J&K's economic backwardness to its status as a conflict area—asserting that in the absence of conflict, its economic progress should have been twice that of HP.

A. Allocations from the Centre

The economic trajectory of the former state of Jammu and Kashmir, spanning the years 1998-2019, is a complex interplay of financial dynamics that have significantly shaped the region's fiscal landscape. Despite the façade of autonomy, the state's economic framework was significantly underpinned by central grants, evident in various financial indicators, which played a pivotal role in the state's economic sustenance.

In the annual financial statement of the 1998-99 year, as reflected in Table, the central grant-in-aid allocation to J&K was estimated at Rs 2,577 crores. During the same period, the state received Rs 1,216.60 crores from the Central

Government as part of the state's share of Union taxes and duties. It included Rs 152.98 in Income Taxes, Rs 1,028.26 crores in Basic Excise Duties and Rs 35.36 crores in Additional Excise Basic Duties for States Tax.[62] While the grant in aid to J&K alone accounted for 57 per cent share of the state's revenue collection for the year, together with the central taxes share, it accounted for 84 per cent of the total revenue collection. On its own, the state could raise a mere Rs 436.61 crores as tax revenue from different sources, including sales tax, land tax, excise and others, whereas a mere Rs 283.25 crores were collected as non-tax revenue like forestry, power and others. This represented a mere 16 per cent of the state's revenue receipts and demonstrated how the state remained very much dependent on the Central Government's largesse despite constant reiterations of its supposedly autonomous character. Table 4.3 shows the year-wise grant in aid delivered to J&K by the Central Government from 1998 onwards till the de-operationalisation of Article 370 on 5 August 2019.

The CAG audit report for J&K for the 1999-2000 financial year reveals that 'the accounts of the State Government closed with a revenue deficit of Rs 400 crores during 1998-99…indicating deterioration in the financial condition of the State Government.'[63] The report further stated that the J&K government, led by CM Farooq Abdullah, has an unsatisfactory record in the quality of expenditure. It castigated the government for burdening the state with liabilities, which rose from Rs 4,602 crores in 1994-95 to Rs 6,835 crores in 1998-99 and marked a 49 per cent increase because of its reliance on borrowings to bridge the financial gap. This was attributed to an 88 per cent rise in internal debt, a 36 per cent increase in loans and advances from the Central Government and a 42 per cent expansion in other liabilities.

Table 4.3 Total Central Government assistance to J&K (1998-2019)

Year	Total Annual Receipts (crores)	Grants-in-aid Amount (crores)	Percentage Revenue Receipts	Central Taxes Share (crores)	Percentage Revenue Receipts	Total Central Assistance (crores)	Percentage of total revenue receipts
1998-99	4509	2577	57	1212	27	3789	84
1999-00	5513	3299	60	1231	22	4530	82
2000-01	5660	3795	67	675	12	4470	79
2001-02	6489	4646	72	576	8	5222	80
2002-03	7548	4965	66	684	9	5649	75
2003-04	8212	5591	68	817	10	6408	78
2004-05	8866	5940	67	934	11	6874	78
2005-06	10315	7017	68	1135	11	8152	79
2006-07	11182	7337	65	1413	13	8750	78
2007-08	13277	8136	61	1775	14	9911	75
2008-09	14302	8955	62	1896	13	10851	75
2009-10	17588	11691	67	1914	10	13605	77
2010-11	22234	14591	65	3067	14	17658	79
2011-12	24782	14541	59	3495	14	18036	73
2012-13	26217	14354	55	3871	14	18225	69
2013-14	27128	13843	51	4142	15	17985	66
2014-15	28938	16149	56	4477	15	20626	71
2015-16	35780	16728	47	7813	22	24541	69
2016-17	41978	20598	49	9489	23	30087	72
2017-18	48512	22701	47	11912	24	34613	71
2018-19	51069	23065	45	13,990	28	37055	73

Source: J&K Government Annual Budget Documents & Annual CAG Reports

Figure 4.1 Trend of central grant-in-aid assistance to J & K (1998-2019) The grant in aid to J&K jumped to Rs 3,299 crores in the financial year of 1999-2000. This represented a 60 per cent share of the state's revenue; and together with its share in the Union taxes, it represented 82 per cent of the revenue. The portion of Union taxes allocated to the state, which includes excise duties and taxes on non-corporate income, saw

Figure 4.1 Trend of central grant-in-aid assistance to J & K (1998-2019)

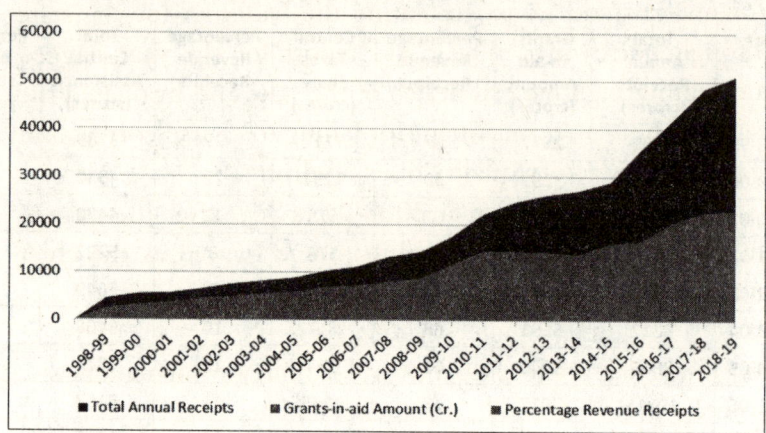

a modest 1.7 per cent increase in the past year. Concurrently, grants-in-aid received from the Central Government surged by a substantial 28 per cent. Nonetheless, when considering total revenue receipts from both sources, their collective share decreased from 84 per cent in 1998-99 to 82 per cent in the fiscal year 1999-2000.[64]

The state government recorded a revenue deficit of about Rs 541 crores for the year, thereby failing to recover from its

Figure 4.2 Annual trend of J&K's share in central tax collection (1998-2019)

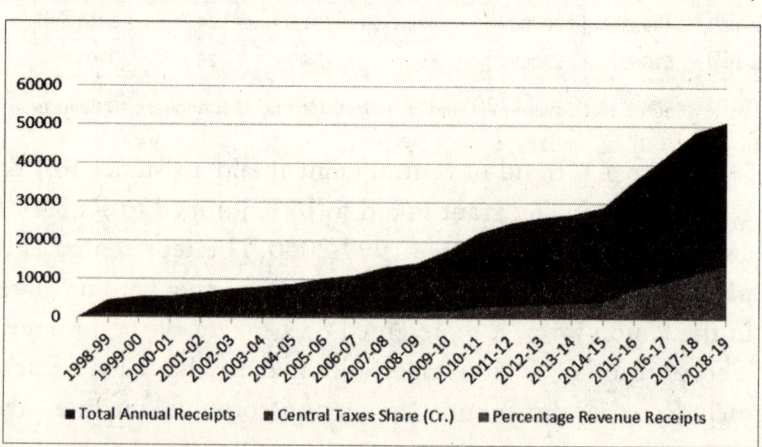

downward trend in accumulating the liabilities for the state through borrowings. The CAG report for the year flagged the debilitating financial health of the state and castigated the Farooq Abdullah government for failing to course-correct and for its unsatisfactory quality of expenditure.[65]

In the financial year of 2003-04, a year after the change in government with Mufti Muhammad Sayeed as the chief minister of the coalition government of People's Democratic Party (PDP) and Indian National Congress (INC), the state continued to grapple with 'the fiscal liabilities' which 'increased from Rs 8,182 crores in 1999-2000 to Rs 13,038 crores in 2003-04 at an average annual growth rate of 13.93 per cent.' At the same time, though, the government managed to show a revenue surplus in its accounts of Rs 458 crores.[66] The state received Rs 5,591 crores as grants-in-aid assistance from the Central Government, with an increase of 12.59 per cent from the previous Rs 4,966 crores in 2002-03. It accounted for 60 per cent of J&K's revenue receipts, and together with its share of Rs 817 crores in the Union taxes, the central assistance represented 78 per cent of the state's total revenue receipts. The further breakdown of the grants-in-aid to J&K included Rs 2,701 crores for the Grants for State Plan Schemes, Rs 2,659 crores as Non-Plan Grants and Rs 231 crores for the Grants for Central, Centrally Sponsored Plan Schemes and Special Plan Schemes.

In the last year of the PDP-INC government led by Ghulam Nabi Azad of INC, which ended in July 2008 with the premature withdrawal of coalition support by the PDP, the overall financial condition of the state during 2007-08, as evident from key indicators such as revenue, fiscal, and primary deficits, shows a blend of trends in the fiscal scenario. While there was an increase in revenue surplus, reaching its highest point at Rs 1,088 crores in 2007-08, both fiscal and primary deficits worsened in comparison to the previous year. The state received Rs 8,136 crores as grants-in-aid, which was 61 per cent of its revenue receipts. Together with the Rs 1775 crores (13.37) as J&K's share in the Central Taxes, it represented 75 per cent of the state's total revenue collection.[67] It is the increase in the additional revenue receipts of the state due to increased grants-in-aid and share in central taxes to the state that explains the J&K government's showing of the record revenue surplus in its accounts for the 2007-08 financial year.

Figure 4.3 Trend of Central Government assistance to J & K (1998-2019)

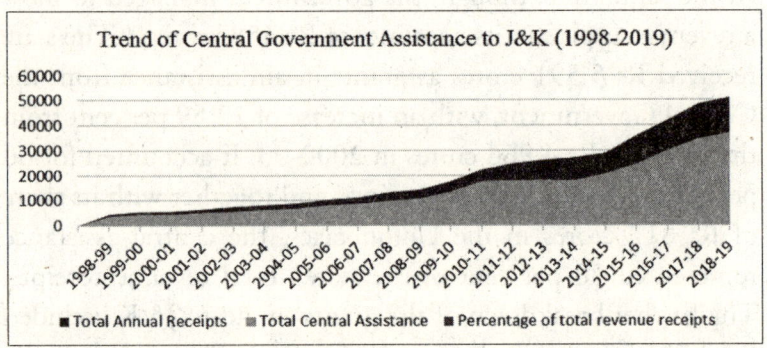

During the 2008-09 financial year, the state received Rs 8,955 crores in grants-in-aid from the Central Government, which is 62 per cent of the total revenue for the year. Additionally, the state received Rs 1,827 crores as part of its share in central taxes, and together with grants-in-Aid, accounted for 75 per cent of the total revenue receipts of J&K.[68] Interestingly, for the first time, the CAG report referred to the funds in addition to the grants-in-aid and central tax share, that the Central Government had been transferring directly to various State Implementing Agencies (SIAs) for different schemes and projects. These funds were not accounted for in

Figure 4.4 Percentage change in Central Government assistance to J & K (1998-2019)

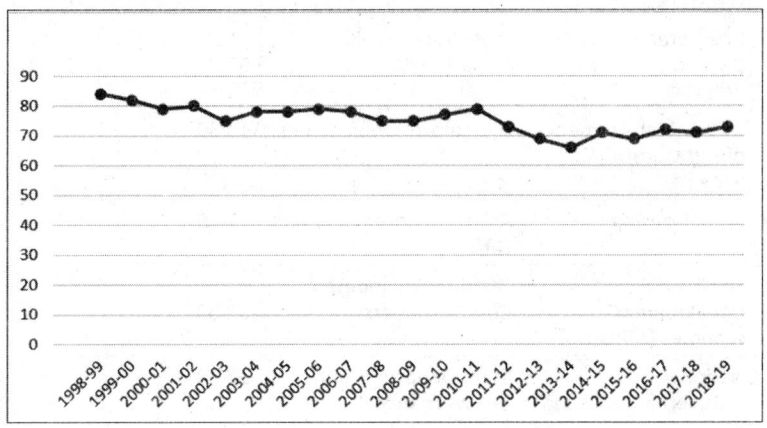

the state's financial statements.[69] For the fiscal year 2008-09, J&K received Rs 1,140 crores through this process. At the same time, the CAG noted that the state government had failed to maintain oversight over these funds, as there lacked a 'consolidated database at the apex level' for its accounting. The breakdown of the direct funds transfer to various SIAs during 2008-09 is shown in Table 4.4.

Table 4.4 Funds transferred directly to State Implementing Agencies during 2008-09 (in crores)

Name of the Programme/Scheme	Name of the Implementing Agency in the State	Total fund released by GOI during 2008-09 (Rupees in crore)
Accelerated Rural Water Supply Programme	SGO Secretary Finance, PHE Department	403.73
National Rural Health Mission (NRHM)	State Health Department and other agencies	64.69
Sarva Shiksha Abhiyan	Ujala Society, Education Department	205.32
NREGS	Assistant Commissioners DRDA	105.36

Pradhan Mantri Gram Sadak Yojana (PMGSY)	State Rural Roads Agency	191.36
Integrated Child Development Programme	State Social Welfare Department	37.92
Macro Management of Agriculture Schemes	Agriculture Department	18.30
Rural Housing (IAY)	Assistant Commissioners DRDA	71.29
Local Area Development schemes (MPLADS)	District Development Commissioners	25.00
National e-Governance Action Plan	State Department for e-Governance	17.28
Total		**1140.25**

Audit Report on State Finances ended 31 March 2009 available at: https://cag.gov.in/webroot/uploads/download_audit_report/2009/Jammu_Kashmir_SF_2009.pdf

In the financial year 2009-10, with the new J&K NC-INC government at the helm of the state led by Omar Abdullah consolidated, the state's accounts demonstrated:

> Huge variations in the revenue surplus, fiscal and primary deficits visàvis their budget estimates. The revenue surplus was less by Rs 2,249 crores than that estimated. The fiscal deficit was Rs 3,989 crores against the estimate of Rs 2,081 crores and primary deficit Rs 1,850 crores, against the estimated Rs 352 crores (March 2010). Reasons for variations between the budget estimates and actual realisation were, however, neither intimated by the Government nor were on record.[70]

The state's revenue receipts show that J&K received Rs 11,691 crores as grants-in-aid from the Central Government, representing 67 per cent of its total revenue. In addition, the state received Rs 1,915 crores as its share from the Central Tax bursary. Together, they accounted for 77 per cent of J&K's total revenue receipts. Further, the Central Government transferred Rs 1,171 crores through many State Implementing Agencies for various schemes/programmes in social and economic sectors. The CAG report for 2009-10 once again censured the government of Jammu and Kashmir for failing to maintain a 'consolidated database at the apex level…to ensure proper accounting of these funds.'[71] A breakdown of the funds released through this mechanism is shown in Table 4,5.

Table 4.5 Funds transferred directly to State Implementing Agencies during 2009-10 (in crores)

Name of the Programme/ Scheme	Name of the Implementing Agency in the State	Direct Funds released by GOI in 200910
Accelerated Rural Water Supply Programme	SGO Secretary Finance	289.90
National Rural Health Mission(NRHM)	State Health Department and other agencies	90.00
Sarva Shiksha Abhiyan	Ujala Society	373.63
Setting up of 6000 model schools at block level		25.82
NREGS	Assistant Commissioners DRDA	173.24
Pradhan Mantri Gram SadakYojana (PMGSY)	State Rural Roads Agency	144.70
Integrated Child DevelopmentProgramme	State Social Welfare Department	
Macro Management of Agriculture Schemes	Agriculture Department	
Rural Housing (IAY)	Assistant Commissioners DRDA	57.25
Local Area Development Schemes (MPLADS)	District Development Commissioners	17.00
National eGovernance ActionPlan	State Department for e-Governance	
Total		**1171.54**

Source: Audit Report on State Finances ended 31 March 2010, at https://cag.gov.in/webroot/uploads/download_audit_report/2010/Jammu_Kashmir_SF_2010.

In the financial year 2014-15, J&K received Rs 16,149 crores as grants-in-aid from the Central Government, accounting for 56 per cent of its total annual revenue receipts. Besides, the state received its share of Rs 4,477 crores from the central tax pool. Together, these accounted for 71 per cent of J&K's revenue.

In the financial year 2018-19, before Article 370 was made de-operationalised from the erstwhile state of J&K and its bifurcation and downgrading to the status of Union Territory, it received a total of Rs 23,065 crores as grants-in-aid from the Central Government, which accounted for 45 per cent of the revenue receipts of the state. Additionally, the state received Rs 13,990 crores as its share from the central tax pool. Together, these accounted for 72 per cent of the total receipts.

Local budgetary allocations

As already highlighted in the preceding sections, the economic journey of the erstwhile State of Jammu & Kashmir during the 1998-2019 period encapsulates a complex narrative of financial reliance on Central Government funds amidst a quest for self-sustained growth. This retrospective analysis draws upon an array of publicly available data, including budget documents and audit reports, to shed light on the profound dependence of the state on central grants. This reliance underscores the challenges the state faces in generating its own resources for sustenance. The trajectory of J&K's self-generated revenue reveals pivotal shifts in its fiscal dynamics.

During this period, the state exhibited a pronounced dependence on Central Government funds to meet its annual budgetary needs. This reliance is evident through the distribution of revenue sources. The composition of revenue receipts witnessed changes, with the state's self-generated revenue from tax and non-tax avenues experiencing marginal increments. From a mere 16 per cent local resource generation in the 1998-99 fiscal year, J&K's self-generated revenue receipts showed slow growth and could only reach a maximum of 34 per cent in the 2012-13 fiscal year. This demonstrates the failure of the state governments to leverage their resources to generate financial capital that could have been used for improving the basic socioeconomic infrastructure of the state.

The erstwhile State of Jammu & Kashmir had been overly reliant on the Central Government funds for meeting the state's annual budgetary allocations. The sources of data over the years such as budget documents and audit reports, as available in the public domain, reveal the pervasive dependence of the state on the financial generosity of the Central Government. This manifested its failure to generate resources for its basic subsistence. The trend of J&K's self-generated revenue is shown in Figure 4.5.

Figure 4.5 Contribution of J & K's self-generated resources to total revenue receipts (1998-2019)

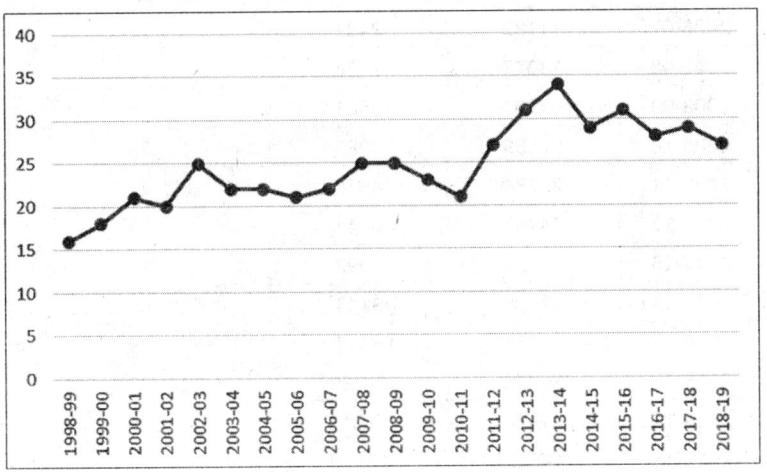

The chart demonstrates that the erstwhile state of J&K has been overly reliant on funds from the Central Government to sustain its budgetary allocation. Interestingly, the local share in the state's revenue receipts never exceeded 34 per cent, which happened during the 2013-14 financial year. Table 4.6 shows the year-wise revenue generated by the J&K Government during the 1998-2019 period. The corresponding trend is shown in Figure 4.6.

Table 4.6 J&K self-revenue receipts

Year	Total Annual Receipts (Rs crores)	State Resources (Rscrores)	Percentage of the total revenue receipts
1998-99	4509	720	16
1999-00	5513	983	18
2000-01	5660	1190	21
2001-02	6489	1267	20
2002-03	7548	1898	25
2003-04	8212	1803	22
2004-05	8866	1992	22
2005-06	10315	2163	21
2006-07	11182	2431	22
2007-08	13277	3326	25
2008-09	14302	3521	25
2009-10	17588	3983	23
2010-11	22234	4576	21
2011-12	24782	6747	27
2012-13	26217	7992	31
2013-14	27128	9143	34
2014-15	28938	8312	29
2015-16	35780	11239	31
2016-17	41978	11891	28
2017-18	48512	13899	29
2018-19	51069	14014	27

Data Source: J&K Government Annual Budget Documents & Annual CAG Reports

In the 1998-99 financial year, the J&K Government generated Rs 720 crores out of the total of Rs 4,509 crores in revenue receipts from autonomous sources such as taxation and non-tax revenue, which is a mere 16 per cent of the state's total receipts. In contrast, a substantial 84 per cent of the revenue receipts comprised shares derived from union taxes, duties, and grants-in-aid extended by the Central Government. This distribution underscores a notable reliance on central transfers and grants, thereby pointing to the failure of the state government to streamline its resource generation.

Further, the State Government's financial records revealed a significant revenue deficit amounting to Rs 400 crores, starkly contrasting the preceding year's surplus of Rs 451 crores. This divergence signifies a discernible decline in J&K Government's fiscal health. The State Government's revenue receipts experienced a decrement from Rs 4,642 crores in the fiscal year 1997-98 to Rs 4,509 crores in 1998-99, reflecting a decrease of approximately 3 per cent. This decline in revenue receipts correspondingly led to a decrease in their relative proportion within the overall receipts, declining from 90 per cent in 1997-98 to 80 per cent in 1998-99.

Figure 4.6 Trend of J & K's self-generated resources revenue receipts (1998-2019)

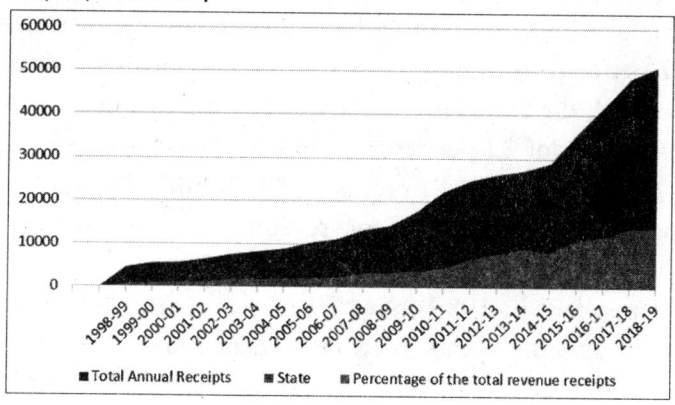

The 1999 report by the Comptroller and Auditor General (CAG), tabled in the state assembly on 10 April 2000, revealed that the expenditure quality of the J&K Government in the fiscal year 1998-99 exhibited suboptimal characteristics, evident through the meagre proportion of Plan expenditure within Revenue and Capital expenditure constituting a mere 11 per cent of the total outlay. It further discerned expenditure inefficiencies in the 'non-remunerative expenditure on incomplete projects and amount of wastages. Diversion of funds and unspent balances under deposits amounted to Rs 138 crores and Rs 105 crores respectively.'

Further, the fiscal deficit, emblematic of the government's net borrowing, witnessed a staggering surge of 675 per cent, escalating from Rs 136 crores in 1994-95 to Rs 1,054 crores in 1998-99. Within this borrowing framework, the fiscal year 1998-99 saw 38 per cent of these acquired funds allocated to offsetting Revenue Deficit, while the remaining 62 per cent were dedicated to fuelling capital expenditures and facilitating loans intended for developmental and other strategic objectives.

At the turn of the millennium, in the financial year of 1999-2000, the share of J&K's self-generated revenue from tax and non-tax avenues increased marginally to 18 per cent from the previous 16 per cent of 1998-99, corresponding with the marginal decrease in the share of the Central Government to 82 per cent from 84 per cent of the previous year. During this period, the State Government's revenue receipts witnessed an increment of 22 per cent, ascending from Rs 4,509 crores in 1998-99 to Rs 5,514 crores in 1999-2000. However, the proportional contribution of revenue receipts within the overall receipts exhibited a slight reduction, declining from 80.11 per cent in 1998-99 to 79.82 per cent in 1999-2000. This underscored the prevailing dependence on central transfers and grants, warranting a deeper examination of its implications for the state government's financial autonomy and stability within the broader fiscal landscape. The J&K Government ended 2000-01 with a notable revenue deficit amounting to Rs 961 crores, marking a significant 77 per cent increase from the preceding year's deficit in 1999-2000. This pronounced increase in the deficit underscored an evident deterioration of J&K's overall financial health.

J&K witnessed a change of government in 2002. Mufti Mohammad Sayeed of the People's Democratic Party (PDP) assumed the reigns of the state government in alliance with the Indian National Congress. The change in the government was seen as a fresh breath in the state, with its promises of bringing peace and development to the state, as J&K strived to emerge from the horrors of Pakistan-sponsored terrorism. Interestingly, the change of government saw a huge turnaround in the state's financial health, with the 2002-03 year recording a revenue surplus of Rs 368 crores before jumping to Rs 458 crores during the 2003-04 year. However, it should be noted that the revenue deficit started witnessing a trend reversal from the 2001-02 fiscal year when it decreased to Rs 334 crores from the previous Rs 961 crores during 2000-01.

During 2003-04, the revenue receipts of J&K were recorded at Rs 8,212 crores, of which the state generated Rs 1,803 crores from its tax and non-tax sources, which accounted for 22 per cent of the state's total revenue receipts against the 78 per cent of the collective contribution of central tax transfers and grants-in-aid. This represented a significant progression from Rs 5,514 crores in 1999-2000, indicating a discernible trend growth rate of 12 per cent. Nevertheless, this growth trajectory also exhibited significant fluctuations between successive years, as the State's Gross Domestic Product (GDP) exhibited an average growth rate of 11.86 per cent during the five-year interval of 1999-2004. The primary contributor to the State's own tax revenue was the sales tax, commanding a majority share of 58 per cent, followed by State Excise (18 per cent), Stamps and Registration Fees (3 per cent), and Taxes on Vehicles (3 per cent). Among non-tax revenue sources, the preeminent contributors were power receipts (58 per cent), interest receipts (19 per cent), and revenues derived from Forestry and Wildlife activities (9 per cent).

The state underwent a political crisis in 2008, with the PDP withdrawing support from the government, which had been led by Ghulam Nabi Azad of Congress since 2005, months before the term of the assembly ended. In the 2007-08 fiscal year, the state recorded a revenue surplus of 1,088 crores, when it contributed Rs 3,326 crores (25 per cent) to the revenue receipts of the government out of the total of Rs 13,277 crores in receipts against the central assistance of Rs 9,911 crores (75 per cent) during the same period.

The major contributors to the state's revenue resources included Rs 1,805 crores in taxes on sales, trade and other such activities, Rs 244 crores in taxes from state excise, and Rs 73 crores in taxes on vehicles, among others.

The elections for the state assembly held in the autumn of 2008 resulted in a divided mandate, which saw Omar Abdullah of the National Conference leading a coalition government in alliance with the Indian National Congress from January 2009 onwards. As such, during the fiscal year of 2009-10, the accounts of the state showed a fiscal deficit of Rs 3,989 crores, nearly double the budget estimates of Rs 2,081 crores. This was the case even as the primary deficit amounted to Rs 1,850 crores, a substantial increase from the projected Rs 352 crores. In terms of revenue collection by the state, it generated Rs 3,983 crores in tax and non-tax revenue, which amounted to 23 per cent of the state's total revenue receipts.

The major contributors to the state's revenue included

Rs 2,146 crores from sales tax, Rs 294 crores from excise collection, Rs 70 crores from the stamps and registration fee, Rs 120 crores in taxes and duties on electricity, and Rs 300 crores in taxes on goods and passengers, among others.

As the tenure of the NC-INC alliance government neared its end in 2014, discernible financial setbacks became apparent within the state's fiscal landscape. This was exemplified by the sliding down of the state's revenue surplus to Rs 70 crores in 2013-14 from the previous Rs 1100 crores in the 2012-13 fiscal year. Interestingly, the government had originally projected a surplus of Rs 5280 crores, as evidenced in the 2013-14 annual financial statement presented in the assembly. Regarding the state's local financial resources, the government disclosed that its internally generated revenue receipts amounted to Rs 8,312 crores, constituting approximately 29 per cent of the total revenue receipts for Jammu and Kashmir during the fiscal year 2014-15. This assessment was made in the context of the overall revenue figure of Rs 28,938 crores.

Following the establishment of the PDP-BJP government in March 2014 and the subsequent rise to power of the BJP-led National Democratic Alliance (NDA) in May 2014, there arose a heightened expectation for a substantial rejuvenation of the state's economy. Notably, both coalition partners had made significant pledges, with particular emphasis on the historic involvement of the BJP in local governance within Jammu and Kashmir.

Despite a notable increase in state revenue receipts from Rs 27,128 crores to Rs 28,938 crores, this surge led to a renewed state of revenue deficit in the fiscal accounts of Jammu and Kashmir, showing a deficit of Rs 391 crores for the year 2014-15. This situation prompted a comprehensive reassessment by the government, resulting in a more modest anticipated surplus of Rs 2,587 crores in the budget projections. However, this anticipated turnaround did not materialise, and instead, the state's finances deteriorated further, with the revenue deficit increasing to Rs 640 crores in 2015-16. Nevertheless, there was a positive development in terms of local resource generation. In the fiscal year 2014-15, the state managed to generate local resources amounting to Rs 8,312 crores. Impressively, this figure saw substantial improvement in the subsequent year, surging to Rs 11,239 crores for the fiscal year 2015-16, constituting 31 per cent of the state's total resources.

The state underwent political uncertainty again in 2018 when BJP withdrew its support from the Mehbooba Mufti-led coalition government. Mehbooba Mufti assumed chief ministership of J&K in 2016 following her father Mufti Muhammad Sayeed's death in 2015 after months of brinkmanship. BJP and PDP had accumulated disagreements on a number of issues, with the BJP criticising Mehbooba Mufti's approach to governance and accusing her of taking unilateral decisions.

The PDP-led government, however, made a comprehensive recovery, which was reflected by J&K reporting a record revenue surplus of Rs 7,596 crores by the 2017-18 fiscal end. This was reversed in 2018-19, with the government implementing the recommendations of the 7th Pay Commission in April 2018.

For the fiscal year 2018-19, the J&K Government fell short of meeting its budget estimates for several key financial aspects, including Revenue Receipts, State's Own Tax Revenue, Non-Tax Revenue, Revenue Expenditure, Capital Expenditure and Total Expenditure. It nevertheless generated local revenues of Rs 14,014 crores in this fiscal year 2018-19, more by Rs 115 crores from the previous year, before the state's bifurcation and the downgrading of J&K into a Union Territory on 5 August 2019. This amount accounted for 27 per cent of the total annual revenue receipts for the fiscal year 2018-19. Overall, the Revenue Receipts and the Total

Receipts showed an upward trend during the 2014-19 period. The composition of the state's revenue receipts is shown in Figure 4.7.

Figure 4.7 Composition of J & K's revenue receipts

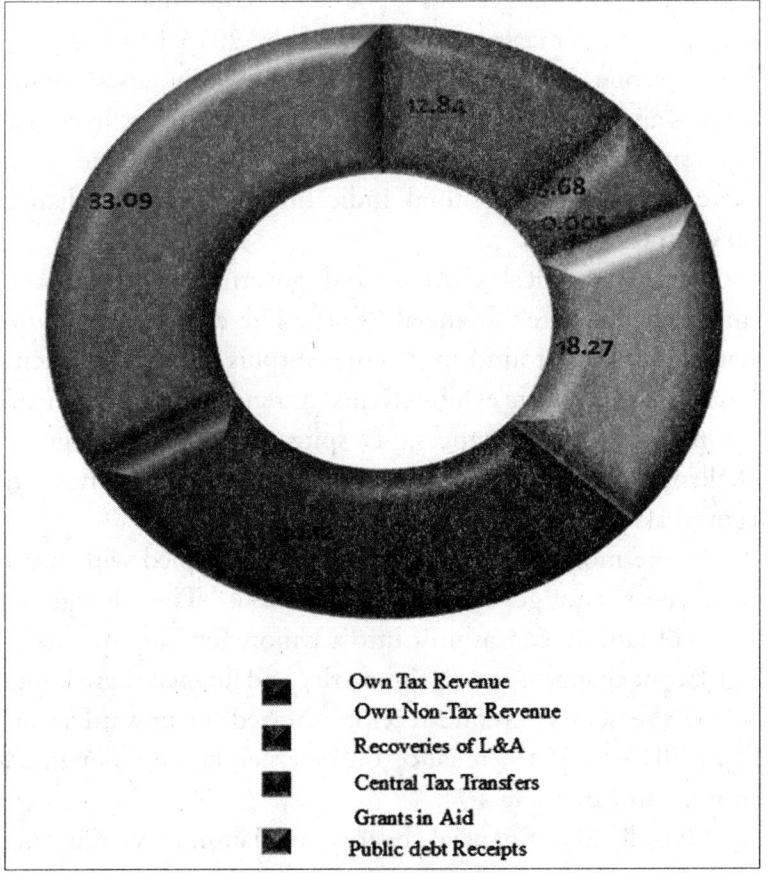

- Own Tax Revenue
- Own Non-Tax Revenue
- Recoveries of L&A
- Central Tax Transfers
- Grants in Aid
- Public debt Receipts

In conclusion, the financial trajectory of the erstwhile state of J&K was marked by a notable reliance on Central Government funds to sustain its budgetary allocations. Over the years, data from various sources, including budget documents and audit reports, highlight the extent of this dependency, revealing the state's struggles to generate sufficient resources for its fundamental needs. The trend of self-generated revenue, as depicted in the charts, underscores the consistent pattern of relying on external financial support.

Throughout its history, the state's revenue makeup has witnessed fluctuations. The local contributions never surpassed 34 per cent, as observed in the 2013-14 fiscal year. The revenue generation breakdown between autonomous sources and central assistance paints a telling picture. In earlier years such as 1998-99, the state's self-generated revenue was a mere 16 per cent of the total, indicating a substantial reliance on central transfers.

Various political changes and government shifts have impacted the state's financial health. The early 2000s saw a remarkable turnaround in revenue surplus and fiscal deficit, but subsequent years exhibited mixed trends, often influenced by political circumstances. Despite periods of progress, challenges persisted, leading to a continuing reliance on central assistance.

In the more recent period, the state grappled with fiscal imbalances and governmental transitions. The change of status of Jammu & Kashmir into a Union Territory marked a significant change in its administrative and financial landscape. While the state's revenue receipts showed an upward trend from 2014 to 2019, reliance on external support remained prominent (see Table 4.7).

Overall, the financial history of Jammu & Kashmir underscored the complexities of maintaining fiscal autonomy and stability, particularly within a region that has experienced political shifts and external influences. The state's journey highlights the ongoing need for strategic resource generation and prudent fiscal management to ensure sustainable development and economic resilience.

Table 4.7 Grant-in-aid provided by the state to autonomous bodies/authorities

Sl. No.	Body/Authority	2014-15 (Cr)	2015-16 (Cr)	2016-17 (Cr)	2017-18 (Cr)	2018-19 (Cr)
1	Srinagar Municipal Corporation	161.16	158.18	285.02	108.47	108.53
2	Jammu Municipal Corporation	108.64	98.54	134.49	163.42	73.80
3	Urban Local Bodies(Kashmir)	87.36	56.03	1.95	105.17	61.63
4	Urban Local Bodies(Jammu)	62.94	76.65	69.61	76.29	46.00
5	SKUAST* – Kashmir	100.54	132.18	166.75	94.62	228.60
6	SKUAST* – Jammu	59.48	54.61	81.00	146.38	101.00
7	Kashmir – University	114.67	156.80	145.84	160.00	211.00
8	Jammu – University	76.14	85.80	124.00	137.00	158.94
9	J&K Sports Council	16.93	19.52	24.55	33.65	34.87
10	J&K Academy of Art andCulture	17.16	15.18	23.97	24.29	18.67
11	Institute of Management & Public Administration (IMPA)	10.47	10.13	12.14	13.70	16.50
12	Khadi and VillageIndustries Board	7.48	17.47	13.11	18.00	23.00
13	Others	446.28	641.59	646.72	1,673.12	2,243.04
	Total	1,269.25	1,522.68	1,729.15	2,754.11	3,325.58

Allegations of Corruption in Jammu and Kashmir

Corruption has been an enduring challenge within the political framework of Jammu and Kashmir. In a region with a complex history and ongoing geopolitical tensions, corruption has penetrated various levels of governance, hindering socioeconomic progress and undermining the trust of its citizens. The state's corrupt political class often peddled the so-called conflict as the *casus belli* of this endemic, which impacted the developmental trajectory of Jammu and Kashmir.

The decades-long corrupt practices by the state's political dispensations bought J&K a reputation as one of the most corrupt states in India. The country's crime watchdog, the National Crime Records Bureau (NCRB), consistently flagged this and ranked the former state of J&K as one of the worst-performing states in India.[72]

The political class on both sides of the divide, the former separatist bloc as well as the mainstream one, had for long nurtured a strong nepotism and patronage network. This network gravely undermined meritocracy and perpetuated corruption. More so, its impact has been the diversion and misappropriation of public funds and resources for personal gain by these politicians, which for long hampered the developmental projects and services meant for the public. It effectively utilised these misappropriated financial incentives and handouts to secure electoral support at the expense of the state's welfare.

Even though the J&K government had established the State Accountability Commission (SAC) under the JK State Accountability Commission Act 2002 as the state's anti-graft body, the Commission remained a toothless institution with merely nominal powers to seek accountability and bring transparency in the system.

For instance, in 2018, the Commission flagged irregularities 'on the implementation of around Rs 1,800 crores worth of Centrally Sponsored Schemes in rural development sector in Jammu and Kashmir.'[73] These included major developmental schemes aimed at transforming the length and breadth of the country, such as Mahatma Gandhi National Rural Employment Guarantee Act (MGNREGA), Pradhan Mantri Awaas Yojana (G), Swachh Bharat Mission (G), National Rural Livelihood Mission, Integrated Watershed Management Programme and Urban Mission. The Commission found a mismatch between governmental claims on the spending of the central funds and the works executed by the departments. It hence sought 'seven-point information along with proof' from the J&K Government:

> The Commission has sought record of the surveys conducted to identify beneficiaries under these six schemes; details of the amount spent under each scheme identifying the beneficiaries and the locations; proof of the job cards supplied and the amount transferred to the beneficiaries' bank accounts under each scheme; proof of the demand made under MGNREGA scheme by the beneficiaries from different areas of the state; whether any supervisory/monitoring mechanism was set up by the Rural Development Department to conduct any physical verification of the works under these schemes, and if any, the particulars of such supervisory body; list of the Ombudsman appointed in 22 districts with all their particulars to enable the SAC to summon them and obtain record on physical execution of various works under these schemes; and details of the Social Audit Unit to be set up along with the details of its operations and reports along with the personnel comprising such Social Audit Unit.[74]

What transpired afterwards is a matter of public record. The state government led by Chief Minister Mehbooba Mufti took away the *'suo moto* power' of the Commission, as stated by the SAC Chairman of the time, Justice (Retd.) Bashir Ahmad Khan, in an interview with *The Print* in 2018. Justice Khan described J&K as 'India's most corrupt' state and lamented that 'there is no political will in the state...to allow efficacy of anti-corruption units.'[75]

Likewise, in 2015, the coalition government of the People's Democratic Party (PDP) and Bharatiya Janata Party (BJP), led by Chief Minister Mufti Muhammad Sayeed, appointed at least 12 judicial officers (out of 22) through its nepotism network in an outright brazen manner. An *Indian Express* investigation expose held that:

> At least 12 of the 22 additional advocate generals, deputy advocate generals and law officers appointed[in June 2015] ...by the Department of Law, Justice and Parliamentary Affairs in Jammu and Kashmir [were] relatives of either ministers or ruling PDP leaders, or of sitting and retired judges, bureaucrats, and even separatist leaders.[76]

What surprised most people in J&K was how the so-called pro-India mainstream political class, which held the governmental reins of the state for decades, actively colluded with the secessionist class, including the militant networks. They did this to sustain the cycle of violence for the region's perpetual instability, which the two blocs exploited for their personal gains. It not only severely undermined the developmental prospects of the state, but also eroded popular trust in government. It weakened the democratic institutions and, by extension, the Central Government, fostering disillusionment and political apathy among citizens. It further undermined the cause of democratic India's mission of accountability and transparent governance across the country by undermining laws.

Further, besides the above cases, some of the infamous scams by the political class include the Jammu and Kashmir Cricket Association (JKCA) scam (Farooq Abdullah), the J&K Bank embezzlement scam (National Conference government), the J&K Bank recruitment scam (People's Democratic Party) and the JKSSB recruitment scams, among others.

J&K Cricket Association Scam

On 10 March 2012, JKCA Managing Committee Chairman, Mohammad Aslam Goni, lodged a First Information Report (FIR) against two office bearers of the cricket body, Ahsan Mirza and Mohammad Saleem Khan, for 'pushing the BCCI funds' meant for the development of sports infrastructure 'into bogus bank accounts created in the name of the association.'[77] Mirza happened to be a close aide of J&K NC patron and former Chief Minister Farooq Abdullah, who served as the president of the cricket body since 2001. The matter reached the J&K Assembly, which witnessed an uproar over the allegations against Farooq Abdullah's corrupt practices as the president of JKCA. The former chief minister of J&K was eventually forced to resign from the sporting body.

With continuous political interference in stalling any headway in the investigation, the J&K High Court finally transferred the case to the Central Bureau of Investigation (CBI) in 2015. [78] The CBI finally chargesheeted Farooq Abdullah and three others in 2018 for 'misappropriating over Rs 43 crores from grants given by BCCI...between 2002 to 2011. The Enforcement Directorate (ED), in a supplementary chargesheet on 26 July 2022, charged the former chief minister for 'irregularities in grants of Rs 112 crores given by the Board of Control for Cricket in India to the Jammu and Kashmir Cricket Association.'[79] The ED claimed that the BCCI grants of over Rs 50 crores were siphoned off under Farooq Abdullah's watch as the president of the state cricketing body. The economic offences body had previously attached properties worth Rs 11.86 crores belonging to Abdullah in December 2020. The ED further accused the J&K NC patron of abusing 'his position as the president of the association and made appointments in the sports body so that the BCCI-sponsored funds could be laundered.'[80]

The ED action against this political heavyweight of the state, which had seemed impossible a few years ago, signifies the change of wind in the Union Territory of Jammu & Kashmir, after the nullification of Article 370 of the Constitution of India, which had hindered the Central Government from initiating any punitive actions against the political elite of the state.

J&K Bank Recruitment Scam

The recruitment process at J&K Bank in 2015-2017 was marred by gross irregularities, as revealed by the former Governor of the state, Satya Pal Malik, in an interview with the *Times Now* channel on 27 October 2018.[81] The bank initiated the process of recruiting 350 Relationship Executives (RE) on 19 March 2015. Though it took more than two years for the bank to declare the final results on 9 March 2017, what was surprising about the selection list to the state's people was the inclusion of 1250 Banking Associates (BAs), apart from the 350 advertised posts for the RE position. The inclusion of BAs in the selection list raised suspicion among the people. Governor Malik's allegations suggested that the bank officials had conspired to manipulate the list in favour of relatives of politicians and their supporters, excluding deserving candidates who had qualified for the exams and interviews.[82]

The revelation of such corruption in the state's largest financial institution shook the faith of the people, especially the unemployed youth who were hopeful of fair opportunities. The incident highlighted the extent of fraud and bribery prevalent in the recruitment process, where candidates without political connections or willingness to give bribes had little chance of securing a job.

Governor Malik alleged that the officials at J&K Bank had conspired to change 'an entire list of 582 selected candidates secretly...to pave way for the appointment of relatives of politicians and their workers.' Governor Malik stated that he was approached by 40 aggrieved candidates who claimed to have successfully 'passed the bank exam and interview' and of being unjustly excluded from the selection list by certain politicians in favour of their relatives and supporters from the respective parties and constituencies.[83] In response to the situation, Governor Malik took action to rectify the injustice done to the aggrieved candidates. He intervened to ensure that all 582 candidates who had qualified for the exams but were excluded from the original list were given appointment letters:

> I called the J&K bank chairman.... and told him I want jobs for these candidates who had qualified the exams. He (the chairman) said this is not the case of just 40 youth, but there are 582 candidates who had qualified exams but didn't get selected. This is the tragedy of Kashmir... there is so much of fraud and those who don't give bribe have no chance of getting a job. I asked the bank chairman to give the youth their due. I also called the finance secretary and finally, a resolution was adopted and all 582 candidates were given appointment letters last week.[84]

This incident serves as a reminder of the importance

of transparency and merit-based selection processes in institutions responsible for recruiting individuals for crucial positions. It also underscores the need for strong mechanisms to prevent corruption and nepotism, especially in public sector organisations, to uphold the faith and trust of the people in the system. Efforts must be made to establish fair and accountable practices to provide equal opportunities to all qualified individuals and to eradicate any form of favouritism or misuse of power in the recruitment process.

Other Scams Related to J&K Bank

The recruitment scandal detailed above was not the only scam that raised questions about the functioning of the state's largest financial institution. It was embroiled in multiple scams over the years in the former state of Jammu and Kashmir. For example, in 2019, the Jammu and Kashmir Anti-Corruption Bureau (ACB) registered a case involving the sanctioning and disbursing of crop loans worth 400 crores, a term loan of 150 crores from the J&K Bank branch in Mahim (Maharashtra), and bill discounting facilities worth 115 crores from the J&K Bank Vasant Vihar (Delhi) branch in favour of Messers REI Agro Limited. The loans were granted 'without tangible securities and in violation of banking norms,' as alleged by the ACB.[85]

With the UT administration taking strong anti-corruption measures, the ACB finally filed a chargesheet against thirty-one individuals after a two-year investigation in June 2021. It claimed that the loans were sanctioned 'with malafide intention in violation of banking norms in order to confer undue benefit upon the promoters of the company and JLGs.' The chargesheet further asserted that the borrower 'had no intention of repaying the loans,' and the primary purpose was to swindle the obtained funds with the active connivance of select bank officials. The investigation revealed that the company and certain private individuals posing as JLGs created fictitious lists of non-existent farmers, diverting the loan funds back to Messers REI Agro Ltd without crediting any farmers' accounts. It added:

> The company with the malafide intention to cheat the J&K Bank hatched a conspiracy with its officers and some private persons representing as JLGs (Joint Liability Groups) created fictitious lists of farmers who were non-existent under each JLG group and got the loan funds credited directly in the accounts of these JLGs who later diverted the funds back to the borrower company M/s REI Agro Ltd without crediting it to any farmers account.[86]

In another scam, the Central Bureau of Investigation (CBI) launched an investigation on 11 November 2021 into the alleged irregularities surrounding the purchase of the Akruti Gold building in Mumbai for Rs 180 crores by J&K Bank in 2010, originally intended for its integrated office. This incident occurred during the tenure of Omar Abdullah as the state's chief minister, and the bank was under the administration of Haseeb Drabu, who later became J&K's finance minister during the PDP-BJP coalition government from 2014 onwards.[87] Subsequently, the Enforcement Directorate (ED) questioned the J&K National Conference (NC) president in April 2022 in connection with the same case.[88]

Likewise, the Enforcement Directorate (ED) conducted a money laundering investigation involving Hilal Rather, son of former Jammu and Kashmir minister Abdul Rahim Rather, linked to a J&K bank fraud case. Abdul Rahim Rather, a former finance minister, is associated with the J&K National Conference (NC) party. The ED filed a money laundering case against Hilal Rather under the Prevention of Money

Laundering Act (PMLA) after taking cognisance of a CBI FIR and an Income Tax Department probe related to an alleged bank fraud of Rs 177 crores. The CBI accused Hilal Rather of engaging in a criminal conspiracy with former officials of J&K Bank to obtain loans worth approximately Rs 177.68 crores in violation of established rules and guidelines.[89]

These scams reveal serious lapses in governance and oversight on the part of J&K Bank, prompting the need for stronger measures to prevent corruption and ensure accountability. The investigations by various agencies have exposed the alleged misuse of power and financial irregularities, underscoring the significance of maintaining transparent and ethical practices within financial institutions and public administration. It is imperative for authorities to take appropriate action against those found guilty, restore public trust and safeguard the integrity of the financial system.

Roshni Act Scam

On 9 October 2020, the Jammu & Kashmir High Court issued a significant order for a Central Bureau of Investigation (CBI) probe into a land distribution scandal involving the former state government and carried out under the well-known Roshni Act. This ruling brought the spotlight back on the largest land scam in J&K, which had been under litigation for almost a decade. Remarkably, the judgment was delivered nine years after the initial petition was filed in 2011. Despite multiple orders from the High Court, the government authorities had not taken any action.

The origin of the scandal lies in the Jammu and Kashmir State Land (Vesting of Ownership to the Occupants) Act, 2001, commonly known as the 'Roshni Act'. The Governor approved this Act on 9 November 2001 and officially published it in *The Gazette of India* on 13 November 2001. It aimed to address the issue of various government lands that had been encroached upon and utilised for various purposes including construction or plantations in orchards. The Act acknowledged the difficulty in evicting encroachers from such lands due to established legal procedures requiring a hearing before eviction, which could potentially cause widespread unrest. Under the Roshni Act, individuals in unauthorised possession of lands until 1990 were granted proprietary rights upon payment of the cost equivalent to the market rates prevailing in the year 1990.

Significantly, the Revenue Department issued the J&K State Land (Vesting of Ownership to the Occupants) Rules, 2007 (also called 2007 Rules in short), claiming authority under Section 18 of the Roshni Act. However, these Rules were published in the official gazette without the legislature's approval, raising questions about their validity. The 2007 Rules introduced a system of differential pricing, with various rebates applied to the statutorily determined land prices. They also outlined provisions for incentives and penalties, but there was no specified occupation period requirement for lands other than agricultural ones.

The Act faced its first legal challenge in 2011, when a petitioner brought to light serious allegations of land grabbing involving influential individuals, including police officers, politicians and bureaucrats who held significant positions in J&K state. The petitioner sought a thorough investigation into these allegations and urged the establishment of a Special Investigation Team (SIT).[90]

Although the Roshni Act was repealed with the implementation of the Jammu and Kashmir State Lands (Vesting of Ownership to the Occupants) (Repeal and Savings) Act, 2018, it exempted all actions already carried out under the Roshni Act.[91]

The 9 October 2020 ruling of a Division Bench of the J&K High Court, comprising then Chief Justice Gita Mittal and Justice Rajesh Bindal, delivered a significant verdict addressing multiple aspects of the case. The Court observed that the rules established under the Roshni Act lacked legislative approval and criticised the officials' inaction in investigating the scams under the Act. The Court reprimanded the state officials for inaction in investigating the scams under the Act, which it asserted 'amounted to serious criminal offences, necessitating inquiry, investigation and criminal prosecutions'. If further asserted, the encroached state land must be retrieved per the law. As a result, the High Court granted a sanction for a high-level CBI probe and ordered the agency to register cases against the individuals found culpable and proceed with the investigation and prosecution accordingly.[92]

The way forward

Despite some positive developments, corruption remains deeply ingrained in J&K, hindering the progress of deserving and qualified individuals. Fortunately, there has been a decline in the number of reported corruption cases, and anti-corruption agencies have taken action against corrupt officials.

To further address the issue, it is essential to adopt a zero-tolerance policy towards corruption, quicken the process of handling corruption-related cases and appoint a Lokayukta to oversee and combat corruption. Good governance, transparency and the right to information should be emphasised to curb corruption effectively in J&K.

Strong measures are required in public service and welfare departments, and the general public must actively support the fight against corruption. With determination and collaboration, there is hope that corruption can be uprooted from J&K, leading to a corruption-free future for the region. The current UT administration has shown a willingness to take corruption and its practitioners head-on and rid the region of this menace once and for all.

Conclusion

In conclusion, the financial dynamics of the former state of Jammu & Kashmir reveal significant reliance on Central Government allocations to sustain its budgetary requirements. The period from 1998 to 2019 witnessed the state consistently receiving a disproportionately high share of central grants, compared to other states, despite its relatively small population size. This dependency on external financial support has been a consistent pattern throughout the state's history, with locally generated revenue never surpassing a certain threshold.

The state's revenue composition has experienced fluctuations over the years, with central assistance playing a pivotal role in bridging the fiscal gap. Despite periods of progress and intermittent improvements in revenue surplus and fiscal deficit, the political changes and external influences that have shaped the region's trajectory have contributed to enduring reliance on central grants.

The more recent transition of Jammu & Kashmir into a Union Territory marked a significant shift in its administrative and financial landscape. While there were glimpses of improvement in revenue receipts, the underlying reliance on external support remained a prevailing feature. This underscores the complexity of maintaining fiscal autonomy and stability within a region characterised by geopolitical tensions and political shifts.

The allegations of corruption within Jammu & Kashmir's

political framework have further compounded the challenges faced by the region. Corruption, deeply ingrained within the governance structure, has hindered socioeconomic progress and eroded public trust. The region's political class, across ideological divides, has perpetuated a culture of nepotism and patronage, diverting public funds and resources for personal gain. This has not only hindered developmental projects and public services but also perpetuated a cycle of electoral manipulation.

Despite the establishment of accountability mechanisms such as the State Accountability Commission, the lack of real enforcement power has limited their impact. Irregularities in implementing major developmental schemes have highlighted the need for stronger measures to combat corruption and ensure transparency in governance. The importance of active public participation and support in the fight against corruption cannot be overstated.

The current Union Territory administration's commitment to addressing corruption and implementing reforms offers hope for a more transparent and accountable future. However, the challenges are multifaceted and deeply entrenched, and therefore their eradication requires sustained efforts and collaboration from various stakeholders. By fostering a culture of accountability, strengthening oversight mechanisms and prioritising the welfare of the region's citizens, Jammu & Kashmir can aspire to break free from the shackles of corruption and realise its full developmental potential. A corruption-free future is not only a possibility but a crucial imperative for the region's growth and prosperity.

Chapter V

Unleashing the Growth Impetus
J&K Since the Repeal of Article 370

ON 5 August 2019, India witnessed one of the landmark events in its post-independence political trajectory. The Indian parliament approved the realignment of the constitutional relationship between the Union of India and the state of Jammu and Kashmir (J&K) by de-operationalising Article 370 of the Constitution of India. This radical departure by Prime Minister Narendra Modi's government from the approach of the previous governments in New Delhi was considered an essential step for rectifying a long-standing constitutional anomaly from the Nehruvian era. It is expected to pave the way for a comprehensive integration of J&K with the rest of the country.[93]

Repeal and Reorganisation

For the above move, the Central Government introduced four crucial bills and resolutions pertaining to J&K in the Lok Sabha, including (i) the Constitution (Application to Jammu & Kashmir) Order, 2019, (ii) the Resolution for Repeal of Article 370, (iii) the Jammu & Kashmir (Reorganisation) Bill, 2019 and (iv) the Jammu & Kashmir Reservation (2nd Amendment) Bill, 2019. The President of India signed the

Constitution Order 2019 on 5 August 2019 to supersede the earlier 1954 order related to Article 370, reflecting an intent to make all central laws applicable to J&K. The government underscored the aspiration of integrating Kashmir with the rest of India and highlighted the pivotal role of repeal of Article 370 in realising this vision.[94]

This constitutional rearrangement paved the way for the administrative restructuring of the erstwhile state into two Union Territories: J&K and Ladakh. The conferring of UT status on Ladakh addresses its long-standing demand for separation from J&K to tread an independent political trajectory within the Union of India. At the same time, , the Central Government committed to re-conferring statehood on J&K at an opportune time ahead.[95] However, it may be noted that even after five years since the re-organisation of the state, the statehood has not been restored till today. However, the Central Government has assured the Supreme Court of India that the statehood would be returned to J&K in future. So far, the elections to the UT legislature have not been held, and it may finally be conducted before 30 September 2024, as ordered by the Supreme Court of India.

Alongside the de-operationalisation of Article 370, the parliament also rendered the constitutional provision for J&K in the Constitution of India vide Article 35A null and void in the same resolution of 5 August 2019. The symbiotic relationship between the provisions mentioned in these two articles had been instrumental in the grant of a special status to J&K since the 1950s. For several decades, many advocates of change in J&K affairs believed that these provisions acted as major impediments towards realising the wholesome developmental potential of the state. In effect, these provisions encouraged a lackadaisical disposition among the local political class, who remained disinclined to vigorously pursue development to safeguard their political interests. This resulted in J&K's lacklustre growth and overwhelming dependence on Central Government's aid, even to sustain its daily expenses, and virtually made it a non-partaker in the country's economic development. The transformation into two Union Territories following the annulment of Article 370 at the very least brought about a significant shift in this dynamic.

J&K had been bearing the brunt of terrorism for over three decades by now. Article 370, in essence, provided an alibi for a few groups in Kashmir, though failingly, to exploit the state's special status as an exclusionary tenet for fuelling and fanning secessionist tendencies among the local populace.[96] As such, it facilitated Pakistan's perpetuation of the cross-border terrorism business, which Pakistan mastered over the decades in Kashmir, bringing ruin to the region. In fact, these exclusionary provisions helped Pakistan-sponsored terrorist groups use J&K as a laboratory for their terror objectives, which occasionally radiated outward to other parts of the country.

There was a significant turnaround in J&K following the 2019 constitutional realignment, as discernible from the declining graph of terror-related incidents in the region (see Table 5.1). For instance, the UT registered a significantly lesser number of terrorism incidents in 2020 compared to the previous year, as revealed by the government in the parliament in March 2021. According to the Ministry of Home Affairs, J&K reported 244 incidents of terrorism in 2020 against 594 in 2019, signifying a qualitative decrease in this trend by an impressive 59 per cent within one year of the annulment of Article 370.

Table 5.1 Number of terrorism incidents (2018-2021)

Year	Number of Terrorism Incidents
2018	614
2019	594
2020	244
2021	229

Data: Annual Reports of Ministry of Home Affairs, Government of India[97]

The changed constitutional status of J&K facilitated the government of India in taking decisive security measures towards neutralising the terror-nurturing ecosystem in the region. With agencies such as J&K Police and the National Investigation Agency (NIA) fully empowered, a few dozen secessionists, who for decades did Pakistan's bidding in Kashmir, have been since arrested and booked under relevant provisions of law for their complicity in facilitating terrorist groups and radicalising Kashmiri youth. Concurrently, the security agencies, led by the NIA, have been able to unmask the trail of terror financing in J&K.[98] These measures have helped dry the material-cum-monetary resources for the sustenance of terrorism in the region, which has been largely contained during the last four years.

Interestingly, NIA's multifaceted investigation into terror financing unveiled a disconcerting nexus between the so-called mainstream regional political entities and Pakistani terrorist networks. This exposure highlighted how a number of local politicians, despite their ostensible allegiance to India's constitutional framework, were found actively abetting anti-India activities. For instance, Waheed Ur Rehman Para, a close confidant of former J&K Chief Minister and president of the People's Democratic Party (PDP), Mehbooba Mufti, was charged with running a clandestine network of stone-pelting gangs and procuring weaponry for terrorists.[99] Besides, Engineer Sheikh Abdul Rashid, a two-time legislator from Langate in North Kashmir's Kupwara district, was revealed to have extensively funded the activities of terrorists in his native district and was accordingly charged under the Unlawful Activities (Prevention) Act (UAPA).[100] Several other examples attest to this proposition.

These measures have acted as a strong deterrent and hence played a significant role in reducing terrorism, local terrorist recruitment and the resultant insecurity in Jammu and Kashmir, which was earlier marked by periods of manufactured 'anti-India' protests and sponsored stone-throwing incidents. This changed dynamic has been testified by multiple reports which show a qualitative shift in the security landscape of J&K. For instance, within the first year following the repeal of Article 370, J&K recorded a decrease by over 40 per cent in the local recruitment into terrorist organisations. With the government's renewed impetus to change the local reality from one of terrorism to one of development, J&K now had the scope to improve its fortunes based on the dynamics of growth and development.[101]

Within this changed ecosystem, the Central Government has since then successfully changed the very nature of popular perception about the role of governance by addressing socioeconomic issues and putting a lid over the corrupt governance practices of successive local governments which ruled the region for decades. It has taken effective measures to address the issues of secessionism, terrorism, nepotism, discrimination and corruption by attacking its sanctuaries and promoters to enable J&K to embark on a new developmental journey.

Journey Since the Repeal of Article 370

The redefining of the constitutional relationship between Srinagar and New Delhi has yielded significant advancements in J&K's socioeconomic status, as evident through various developmental indicators. The outcomes include empowering the local populace, abolishing discriminatory laws and implementing fair measures to address historical inequalities. In this context, the previously inapplicable central laws such as the Right to Education, Prevention of Child Marriage and Untouchability Act were finally extended to J&K. Additionally, property rights were restored to women, permitting them to acquire real estate and transfer property to their offspring.

A noteworthy amendment to the domicile rules allowed the husbands or spouses of native women holding domicile status in the Union Territory also to seek domicile certificates. This adjustment was instrumental in rectifying a historical disparity on the basis of gender, as previously the non-domicile husbands were ineligible to apply for domicile rights, while non-domicile wives could do so.[102]

At the same time, the government has been able to alleviate the concerns of the people about safeguarding their means of and resources for livelihood. For instance, one of the foremost concerns among J&K residents, following the withdrawal of Article 370, was with regard to the job prospects of local unemployed youth in the UT's government sector. There were apprehensions that this new dynamic could allow non-local candidates to partake in the J&K government's recruitment processes at the expense of local candidates. Cognizant of limited government job avenues, the Central Government in April 2020 issued a landmark order reserving all government jobs within J&K for the UT domiciles.[103] This order demonstrated that the Central Government was in no way interested in putting the locals at a disadvantage in terms of employment opportunities and access to resources, something that had made many sceptical about the intentions of the government.

These changes have collectively propelled comprehensive progress, guiding the region towards a more peaceful and prosperous state. The state has ever since seen a major improvement in the law-and-order situation, as demonstrated by the receding number of terror acts, stone-pelting incidents and other secessionist activities. For instance, a report by J&K Police in 2023 stated that the UT marked a 'remarkable' turnaround in law and order situation and security dynamics, with a substantial reduction in occurrences of stone-pelting and terror-related incidents following the annulment of Article 370. It stated that 'the pre-Article 370 period recorded 5,050 incidents, which significantly reduced to 445 in the post-Article 370 period, marking a remarkable 92 per cent decrease.'[104] Further, according to the Ministry of Home Affairs (MHA) data, the J&K witnessed 618 instances of stone-pelting from January to July 2019, which decreased to 222 during the same period in 2020 and further down to 76 in 2021, as reported by the *Indian Express*.[105]

In terms of terrorism, in contrast to the 930 instances of militancy-related incidents that shook the erstwhile state during the three years preceding the repeal of Article 370, only 617 such occurrences were documented in the three years following the annulment. Further, the count of active militants was 'brought down to double digits' in 2022 from 250 by the close of 2019. Additionally, the recruitment of local youth into militant groups was significantly brought down with active civic engagement. After 206 youths joined the militant ranks in 2018 and 143 in 2019, it came down to 100 in 2022. This, as per J&K Police, demonstrated 'a decline of 37 per cent' from 2021. What is more significant in these figures is that the security agencies neutralised 65 of these new terror recruits and arrested 17 others, and therefore just 18 are still active.[106]

In terms of casualties for the state, police data reveals that from 5 August 2019 to 4 August 2022, 174 police and security personnel were killed in terrorism-related violence, which is a decrease from the 290 personnel who lost their lives in the three years before the repeal. In terms of civilian casualties in such violence, the figures have witnessed a qualitative decline in these years. The UT government data reveals that '110 civilians were killed in the three years following the revocation of Article 370, while 191 civilians lost their lives in militancy violence in the three years preceding the abrogation.'[107]

As such, in terms of improving the lives of the people, the UT administration has been revamped to ensure that the previous obstacles are eliminated, so that people-friendly policies are undertaken to allow the establishment of new businesses and industries, something that people have appreciated. As such, signs of progress include rapid development, improved socioeconomic indicators, significant tourist influx and increased industrial investment.

To take the dividends of the grassroots democracy to the last person of the region, the government of the Union Territory of Jammu and Kashmir has undergone a notable shift in power allocation and resource distribution, empowering newly strengthened Panchayati Raj institutions such as *panches* and *sarpanches*, Block Development Councils, and District Development Councils.[108] This has laid the groundwork for a robust three-tier system of grassroots-level democracy. It is well-known that the Panchayati Raj Institutions in the former state of J&K, operating under the Panchayati Raj Act 1989, lacked authority and remained largely symbolic. The first Panchayat elections in 2011 did not effectively improve its governance structure. With the removal of the constraints of Article 370, the applicability of the 73rd Constitutional Amendment Act of 1992, governing PRIs across India, extended to the UT. Since then, J&K has witnessed a gradual enhancement in the devolution of power to these local self-governance units, which are expected to play a vital role in its development. The commitment of New Delhi toward enhancing grassroots democracy is evident in the release of Rs 800 crores of funds to PRIs in J&K between March and August 2019, followed by another Rs 1200 crores in September 2019.[109]

Similarly, Block Development Councils (BDCs) and District Development Councils (DDCs) were established with financial provisions to further decentralise governance in the region. The first-ever DDC elections in 2020 made these bodies crucial stakeholders in the UT's development trajectory. Interestingly, the 2021-22 budget earmarked Rs 200 crores for J&K's DDCs (Rs 10 crores each), as was unveiled by Finance Minister Nirmala Sitharaman in the parliament on 17 March 2021.[110]

Apart from the improved security dynamics, the de-operationalisation of Article 370 altered the political landscape and the traditional style of politics in J&K perhaps for ever. This was the boldest attempt yet to change the political narrative and bring developmental issues to the forefront of the political discourse. The region had historically been dominated by a select few political families such as the Muftis and the Abdullahs on the one hand and the Hurriyat secessionists on the other hand, both of whom often leveraged the state's autonomous character under Article 370 for their political gains. However, the constitutional rearrangement disrupted this status quo, pushing every political actor since then to re-invent their politics and frame their political discourses accordingly, based on the broader developmental imperatives of the region. With improved governance driving the all-round development of J&K with a positive impact on the lives of locals, the people increasingly realise how the political elite exploited identity politics to safeguard their vested interests at the expense of J&K's developmental requirements in the 21st century. To the political actors, it has now become evident that the earlier-practised deviant rhetoric is a thing of the past. Hence they need to construct their political narratives around the real developmental issues affecting the people, so that they can effectively participate in the political process of the UT. Else, they should be ready to be junked by the masses.

Therefore, it can be safely argued that the events following the revocation of Article 370 on 5 August 2019 marked a significant turning point for total integration of J&K with the Indian Union. The comprehensive transformation carried out by the Government of India has notably shifted popular perceptions about governance by addressing socioeconomic concerns, eliminating long-standing corrupt practices and rectifying historical disparities. By addressing the challenges of corruption and disparity in allocation of funds for different regions within the UT, the government has effectively altered the developmental trajectory of the whole of J&K. This transformation is reflected in remarkable advancements in regional socioeconomic indicators, including empowerment of the local population, eradication of discriminatory laws and equitable measures to address historical inequalities.

These collective changes have led to holistic progress, guiding both regions toward a more harmonious and prosperous future. J&K's economic prospects have been revitalised, attracting external investments through policy measures that encourage economic growth and industrial development. A host of reforms, including memoranda of understanding (MOUs) with various companies, earmarked funds and industrial transformation schemes, have demonstrated collective commitment to fostering economic prosperity in the regions. Moreover, grassroots democracy has been rejuvenated through empowered Panchayati Raj Institutions, BDCs and DDCs, reflecting a robust three-tier local governance system.

The improved security situation has helped reestablish the region as a prominent tourist destination, reversing years of decline and aligning it once again with international tourism circuits. This is evident in the substantial growth in the UT's tourism sector, with a marked increase in the arrival of both domestic and foreign tourists over the last three years. J&K has, for all practical purposes, embarked on a path of progress with a promising future and is aligned with India's journey toward sustainable growth and harmonious integration.

Overview of J&K's Macro Economic Indicators

The Union Territory of Jammu and Kashmir has maintained a consistent share in India's GDP since the fiscal year 2014-15, closely aligning with its population share. Despite contributing 0.8 per cent to the national GDP relative to its 0.98 per cent population share, the region's share remains constant. The Gross State Domestic Product (GSDP) of J&K is projected to grow by 15 per cent in 2023-24, which is in line with the national average. Over the period from 2014-15 to 2021-22, J&K's economy exhibited positive growth with a compound annual growth rate of 6.0 per cent, surpassing the national average of 5.37 per cent. Table 5.2 and Figure 5.1 show the growth trend in J&K's GSDP from 2014-15 to 2022-23 period, demonstrating that the GSDP at current prices witnessed Compounded Annual Growth Rate (CAGR) of 10.88 per cent, whereas the GSDP at constant price (base year 2011-12) grew at the CAGR of 6 per cent during this period. This shows that the economy of the UT has taken the right path, and with the inflow of investments worth thousands of crores committed through hundreds of MOUs with various entities in recent years, it will only expand the volume of the economic activities, thereby unleashing all-round development in the region.

Table 5.2 GSDP of J&K (in crores)

Year	GSDP (at current prices)	Growth Rate	GSDP (at constant price 2011-12)	Growth Rate
2014-15	98367	2.88	82372	-3.22
2015-16	117168	19.11	97001	17.76
2016-17	124848	6.55	100198	3.30
2017-18	139658	11.90	106624	6.41
2018-19	160464	14.42	115061	7.91
2019-20	164135	2.67	113943	-0.97
2020-21	170382	3.70	112628	-1.15
2021-22	195458	14.48	121546	7.92
2022-23	224796	15.01	131294	8.02
CAGR	10.88%		6.00%	

Data taken from Economic Survey of the UT of Jammu and Kashmir 2023

The service sector contributes significantly to the economy, constituting around 64 per cent of the Gross State Value Added (GSVA) in 2022-23 and employing 31 per cent of the workforce. This sector holds substantial growth potential and is essential for overall economic expansion. Despite being consumption-driven with high transportation costs, J&K's 2022 inflation rate of 6.88 per cent is nearly at par with the national rate of 6.69 per cent. Monthly trends show a decrease from 8.17 per cent in January 2022 to 3.74

Figure 5.1 Trend of J&K's GSDP growth rate

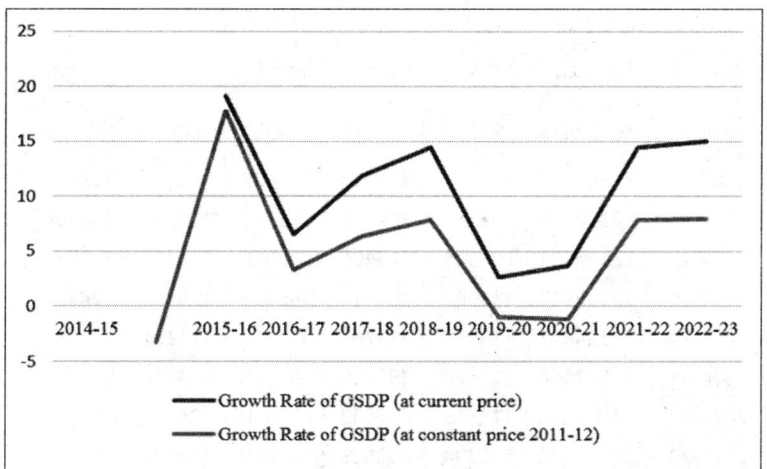

per cent in December 2022, with the Consumer Price Index for agricultural labourers in J&K same as the national average (1167) in December 2022.

In the 2022-23 fiscal year, J&K's nominal GSDP was estimated at around Rs 2.25 lakh crores, with real GSDP at about 1.31 lakh crores. The real GSDP is projected to grow at 8.0 per cent and the nominal GSDP at 15.01 per cent. The Compound Annual Growth Rate (CAGR) of nominal and real GSDP between 2014-15 and 2022-23 is 10.88 per cent and 6.00 per cent respectively. The share of GSDP of J&K and Himachal Pradesh to the All India GDP remained constant at around 0.80 per cent between 2014-15 and 2021-22.

A positive trend is evident when comparing J&K's growth performance to India and the other northern states from 2014-15 to 2022-23. Table 5.3 compares J&K's GSDP with the GSDP of the neighbouring states and the national GDP.

J&K's economy grew at a CAGR of 6.0 per cent, outpacing the national average of 5.37 per cent and three other northern states (see Figure 5.2). These include Punjab (4.78 per cent), Delhi (5.4 per cent) and Himachal Pradesh (5.3 per cent).

Table 5.3 Comparison of GSDP (at constant prices) of J&K with neighbouring states

Year	All India	J&K	Punjab	Delhi	HP	Haryana
2014-15	10527674	82372	312125	428355	89060	370535
2015-16	11369493	97001	330052	475623	96274	413405
2016-17	12308193	100199	352721	511765	103055	456709
2017-18	13144582	106624	375406	542015	109406	482036
2018-19	13992914	115062	397019	565327	116411	524171
2019-20	14534641	113943	413295	587316	121168	566034
2020-21	13687118	112628	399780	564669	114814	536226
2021-22	14925840	121546	427543	622430	124400	588771
2022-23	16000500	131294	453623	652649	134576	630573
CAGR	5.37%	6.0%	4.78%	5.40%	5.30%	6.87%

Source: Economic Survey 2022-23, Government of the UT of Jammu & Kashmir

Figure 5.2 Comparison of J&K's CAGR of GSDP (at constant price) with neighbouring states

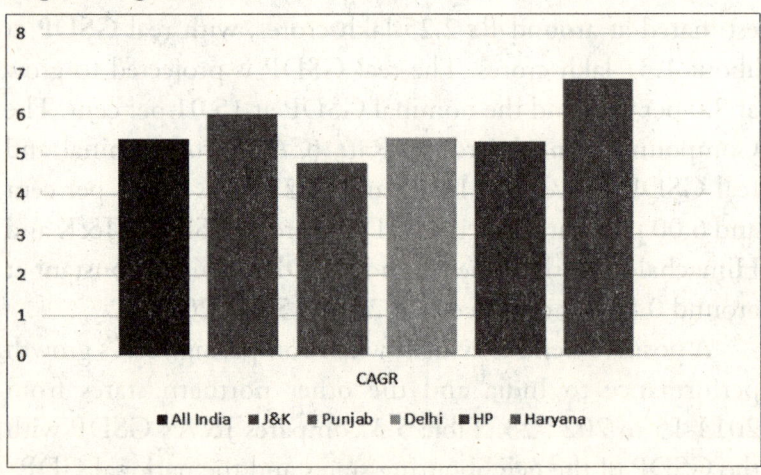

Only Haryana, with a CAGR of 6.87 per cent, outpaces J&K in this indicator.

Furthermore, the per capita income in the Union Territory (UT) is on a rapid growth trajectory, catching up to the national average. Per capita income is a key indicator of economic welfare, reflecting the average income and living standards of a region's population. Although the per capita Gross State Domestic Product (GSDP) and Net State Domestic Product (NSDP) in Jammu and Kashmir (J&K) are currently lower than the national figures, the gap has been diminishing over time. In 2014-15, J&K's per capita NSDP was about 72 per cent of the per capita Net National Income (NNI) at the All-India level. By 2022-23, this ratio has improved to around 77 per cent of per capita NNI.

The compound annual growth rate (CAGR) of per capita income in J&K over the past 8 years is 9.4 per cent, higher than the national level of 8.0 per cent. Even during the challenging year of 2020-21, marked by the COVID pandemic, J&K's per capita income grew by 0.9 per cent, showcasing the UT's economic resilience compared to decline in India as a whole by -4.0 per cent.

Analysing the growth of J&K's per capita income compared to the other northern states from 2014-15 to 2022-23, the trend is positive and accelerating (see Table 5.4). During this period, J&K's per capita income grew at a compound annual growth rate of 8.15 per cent, surpassing the rates of Punjab (6.01 per cent), Delhi (7.62 per cent), and Himachal Pradesh (7.64 per cent), lagging behind only Haryana (9.14 per cent).

In sum, the Union Territory of Jammu and Kashmir has demonstrated consistent progress in expanding its economic dividends while contributing to the country's GDP, close to its population share. Over the years, and more so after 2019-20, J&K's economy has exhibited positive growth, as revealed by the data above. The region's economy is progressing on a

Table 5.4 Comparison of per capita income (at current prices) of J&K with neighbouring states

Year	J&K	Punjab	Delhi	HP	Haryana
2014-15	62327	108970	247209	123299	147382
2015-16	74950	118858	270261	135512	164963
2016-17	78960	128780	295558	150290	184982
2017-18	87710	139835	318323	165497	208437
2018-19	98738	149974	338730	174804	223015
2019-20	101891	154385	356151	185728	240507
2020-21	102803	149894	344136	183333	235707
2021-22	116619	162112	401982	201854	274635
2022-23	132806	173873	444768	222226	296685
CAGR	8.15	6.01	7.62	7.64	9.14

Source: Economic Survey 2023 of J&K and budgetary documents of the compared states.

favourable trajectory, driven by its burgeoning services sector, holding promising potential for further expansion.

Comparing J&K's growth performance to India and the other northern states, it emerges as a positive trend. J&K's economy has maintained a CAGR of 6.0 per cent over this period, outpacing the national average of 5.37 per cent and surpassing several other northern states. Furthermore, the per capita income in the UT has been rapidly advancing towards the national average, signifying growing economic welfare. Despite the per capita GSDP and NSDP being lower than the national figures, J&K has consistently narrowed the gap over time. This trend is reinforced by the per capita income's CAGR of 9.4 per cent over 8 years, even during the challenging year of 2020-21 because of the Covid pandemic. J&K's per capita income growth is prominent compared to other northern states, indicating a promising trajectory for the region's economic progress.

Developmental Allocations from the Central Government

The first budget for Jammu & Kashmir after it was reorganised as a Union Territory was presented by the Union Finance Minister Nirmala Sitharaman on 17 March 2020. It was a supplementary budget necessitated by applying the J&K Reorganisation Act and the official bifurcation of the erstwhile state into UT of J&K and UT of Ladakh on 31 October 2019. The State Administrative Council (SAC), led by the Governor, had earlier worked out the J&K state budget for 2019-20. It estimated the state's revenue collection at Rs 71,193 crores, against the 2018-19 fiscal actuals of Rs 51,069 crores. The same had to be revised for the period 1 March 2019 to 31 October 2019 to Rs 27,738 crores. The supplementary budget for the remaining five months of the 2019-20 fiscal year revised the estimates for the period between 31 October 2019 and 30 March 2020 to Rs 40,498 crores.

Overall, J&K ended the 2019-20 fiscal year with actual revenue receipts of Rs 52,618 crores, with a revenue deficit of Rs 346 crores and a fiscal deficit of Rs 10,679 crores. The revenue receipts of the UT reveal that the resources from the Central Government, including grants-in-aid and share in central taxes, constituted Rs 32,090 crores and Rs 6,802 crores respectively. Collectively, the central resources constituted around 74 per cent of the state's total revenue receipts. The remaining 26 per cent came from locally generated resources, including Rs 9,467 crores in tax and Rs 4,259 crores in non-tax revenue respectively.

The first full-time budget for the Union Territory presented in the parliament was the 2020-21 annual financial statement presented by Union Finance Minister Nirmala Sitharaman on 17 March 2021. The FM emphasised the 'need to fast-track development to meet the aspirations of the people' and hence sought to present a budget that upholds the government's commitment 'to peace, progress and prosperity of the people of J&K.'[111] The government expressed confidence that J&K's 2020-21 fiscal budget would exceed Rs 1 lakh crores mark for the first time, it's the highest ever allocation for J&K, which will transform the UT into a model of development. The total budget estimates amounted to Rs 1,01,428 crores, with developmental spending accounting for around Rs 38,764 crores, thereby reflecting a 27 per cent increase. The budget set the target of 11 per cent Gross State Domestic Product (GSDP) growth that would position the UT among the fastest-growing regions in terms of development.

The Central Government gave itself a broad mandate in the 2020-21 budget, given its objective of justifying the change of status of J&K state and its bifurcation into two Union Territories of J&K and Ladakh. Some of the key promises made by the government included:

A. Rural Sector
  1. 350 lakh days of wage employment to be created.
  2. 7,00,000 households to be employed by MGNREGA.
  3. 90,000 rural assets to be created (playgrounds, drains, protection walls, cremation sheds, etc.).
  4. 64,899 unemployed youth to be provided with skill training.
  5. 2,09,500 women to be brought under the fold of 20,950 SHGs and to be provided Rs 31.42 crores as revolving fund.

B. Agriculture/Horticulture
   1. CA storage capacity to be increased up to 1.70 MTs.
   2. An area of 355 hectares to be brought under High Density Plantations.
   3. Five satellite markets are to be made functional in addition to 17 existing markets.
   4. 1.5 lakh farmers to benefit by increasing the productivity of paddy and maize.
   5. The productivity of the saffron crop will increase to 4.5 kg/Ha as against 4kg/Ha (2019-20) with assured irrigation.
   6. 500 hectares would be utilised for the popularisation of aromatic plants.
C. Tourism
   1. Rs 560 crores provided for the creation and up-gradation of tourism infrastructure.
   2. Rs 40 crores as additional support provided for the promotion of tourism.
   3. 1000 crores to be spent on tourism infrastructure projects under the Prime Minister's Development Programme.
D. School Education
1. 352 schools to provide vocational education to fill the gap between educated and employable and reduce the dropout rate at the secondary level, benefitting 23000 students.
2. 175 ICT labs and 224 CAL centres for Technology Mediated Learning (TML) and Information Communication Technology (ICT/CAL) to expose schoolgoing children to modern technologies under the digital initiative.
E. Science and Technology
   1. Establishment of a sub-regional science centre.
   2. Establishment of state spatial data infrastructure centre (Geo-portal).

3. Establishment of medicinal and aromatic plants demonstration farms.
4. Setting up of liquid chromatography mass spectroscopy (LCMS) units.
5. Establishment of Industrial Biotechnology parks.
6. Providing 20,000 solar street lights @ 1000 SSLS per district under the Decentralised Solar PV Application Scheme.

F. Building Infrastructure
1. Rs 310 crores set aside for the road sector, benefitting 1.65 lakh persons.
2. Construction of 48 bridges benefiting 1.60 lakh persons.
3. Improvement of Mughal Road as an alternate route connecting Jammu & Kashmir.
4. 150 e-buses to be purchased for an eco-friendly urban transportation system.
5. Creation of Mass Rapid Transit Corporation (MRTC) for Jammu and Srinagar to improve urban transport system; Rs 4 crores proposed for each such corporation.
6. Rs 100 crores set aside to restore the health of J&KRTC.
7. Rs 50 crores to encourage the private sector to replace old and unsafe buses.
8. Rs 75 crores provisioned to improve the public transport system.

The 2020-21 budget estimated the revenue receipts for J&K at Rs 91,100 crores and capital receipts of Rs 10,329 crores, as the government claimed that the UT revenues would cross Rs 1 lakh crores. However, the actual receipts of the UT, as revealed by the 2021-22 Annual Financial Statement subsequently, were Rs 67,418 crores, of which Rs 52,495 crores were revenue receipts and the rest Rs 14,923 crores as capital receipts, thereby showing a significant overestimate by the Union Government.[112] The Revenue Receipts fell short by Rs 38,604 crores, Own Tax Revenue by Rs 4,364 crores, Share of Union Taxes by Rs 15,200 crores, Additional Resource Mobilisation by Rs 4,000 crores, and Grants-in-Aid from the Government of India by Rs 15,052 crores compared to the projected budget estimates. Consequently, the Union Territory of Jammu and Kashmir experienced a revenue deficit of Rs 138 crores, a significant deviation from the anticipated revenue surplus of Rs 28,436 crores outlined in the budget estimates.[113]

Regarding the central assistance, the UT received a total of Rs 39,542 crores as revenue receipts from the Union Government, including the grants-in-aid and tax share, and PMDP. This constituted 75 per cent of the total revenue receipts, with the rest of the resources generated locally in the form of tax and non-tax revenue (see Figure 5.3).

Figure 5.3 J&K's revenue receipts (2020-21)

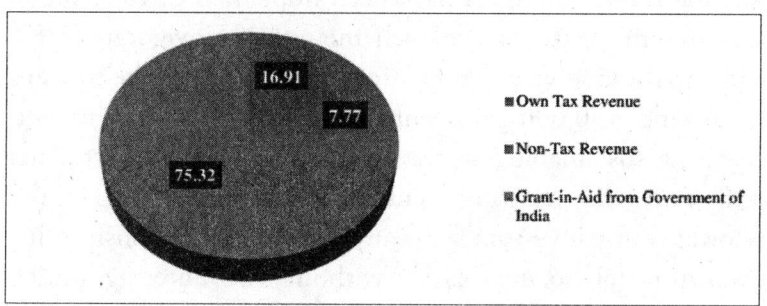

In the 2021-22 budget, presented by Union Finance Minister Nirmala Sitharaman on 17 March 2021, the government emphasised effective measures to deliver good governance, fast-tracking socioeconomic and infrastructure development and creating avenues of employment generation as its priority. The government claimed that the UT made exceptional strides towards financial transparency, with the successful implementation of the Budget Estimation, Allocation and Monitoring System (BEAMS) ushering in an era of openness. BEAMS allows for the efficient release of funds tied to specific activities, revolutionising financial management.

For ushering in industrial development in the region, the Ministry of Commerce Government of India announced the launch of the New Central Sector Scheme for Industrial Development, backed by a substantial allocation of Rs28,400 crores.[114] This initiative aims to foster industrial growth in underserved regions while bolstering existing industries within the state. A central objective of this scheme is to fuel employment generation, thereby spurring socioeconomic advancement throughout the region. The plan also envisions the expansion of both manufacturing and service sector units within J&K. Notable incentives such as Capital Investment, Interest Subvention, GST-Linked Incentives and Working Capital Interest Support have been implemented to facilitate this growth. At its core, this scheme seeks to invigorate J&K's industrial and service sectors, strongly emphasising the creation of around 450,000 jobs, enhancing skill development and fostering sustainable progress by attracting fresh investments and nurturing existing ventures. Of significance is the allowance for investors from any location to establish units, even privately owned land, without encountering undue obstacles in ownership transfers. This initiative signifies a pivotal milestone in J&K's journey toward industrial development. On a broader scale, the Government of J&K identified 14 sector-specific policies to attract investors, complemented by adequate land resources.

The budget estimates for the 2021-22 fiscal year put the

total receipts of J&K at Rs 1,08,621 crores, including the revenue receipts of Rs 97,141 crores and capital receipts of Rs 11,480 crores, with a projected revenue surplus of Rs 28,337 crores. The Revenue Receipts of Rs 59,238 crores showed a 13 per cent growth compared to the previous year, which was, however, substantially short of the budgeted estimates of Rs 97,141 crores by 39 per cent. This demonstrates that the government was unable to adhere to the budget's defined targets for both Fiscal Deficit and Primary Deficit. J&K experienced a significant rise of 32 per cent in its tax revenue and 19 per cent in non-tax revenue compared to the preceding year. This led to an overall increase in Revenue Receipts by Rs 6,742 crores. Despite the optimistic projection of a Revenue Surplus amounting to Rs 28,337 crores, the actual outcome for the year revealed a Revenue Deficit of Rs 31 crores, which was marginally lower than the previous year's Rs 138 crores.[115]

The Union Finance Minister Nirmala Sitharaman presented the 2022-23 budget for J&K on 22 March 2022 in parliament. The government emphasised that the budget aimed at consolidating good governance in the UT, facilitating the investment and industrial growth for accelerated development and inclusive growth to improve the life quality, deepen the grass-root democracy, generate employment avenues and, importantly, undertake women's empowerment initiatives. The finance minister claimed that the UT governance had undertaken 'financial prudence, transparency and zero tolerance to corruption,' which had "enhanced financial inclusion and social equity":

> Several important reforms have been undertaken to ensure transparency and accountability in the administration. Today a fear-free, corruption-free system of governance has been established through a paperless, faceless procedural framework. No work is allotted without following tendering

process and without having Administrative Approval/ Technical sanction. No bill is passed without geo-tagging of photographs through PROOF (Photographic Record of On-site Facility) application and physical verification of works. Every single penny is now spent for the welfare of the people.[116]

The Central Government further claimed that after the de-operationalisation of Article 370 in August 2019, Jammu and Kashmir achieved a significant milestone by introducing the District Good Governance Index, making it the pioneer among all States and Union Territories in the country. This index aims to evaluate the effectiveness of the public service delivery system at the district level, with the purpose of enhancing transparency to fulfil people's desires.

The government projected the 2022-23 budgetary estimates for J&K at over Rs 1 lakh crores, signifying a strong commitment to transforming the region into a development model for the country. The total estimated budget for the year was projected at Rs 1,12,950 crores (net) out of a gross budget of Rs 1,42,150 crores (which included a Ways and Means Advance of Rs 29,200 crores). Out of this, approximately Rs 41,335 crores is allocated for developmental expenditures of the UT. The total estimated budget included Revenue Receipts of Rs 1,02,322 crores and Capital Receipts of Rs 10,628 crores, with the Revenue Surplus and Fiscal Deficit being Rs 30,707 crores and Rs 9,570 crores respectively. It further estimated a significant rise in the capital component of the budget designated for infrastructure development initiatives.

In the context of developmental allocation across different areas, a breakdown of budgetary allocations in capital expenditure for the fiscal year 2022-23 reveals the following figures: Rs 1,950.04 crores designated for the Agriculture and

Horticulture Sectors (an increase of Rs 310.08 crores from the previous year's allocation), Rs 391.90 crores for the Animal, Sheep Husbandry and Fisheries Sectors (a rise of Rs 38.86 crores from the previous year's allocation), Rs 1,806.66 crores for Education (an increment of Rs 249.17 crores from the previous year's allocation), Rs 1,484.72 crores for Health and Medical Education Sector, Rs 4,627.85 crores for Rural Economy (an increase of Rs 327.40 crores from the previous year's allocation), Rs 604.77 crores for Tourism and Culture (an augmentation of Rs 78.61 crores from the previous year's allocation), Rs 5,217.87 crores for Road Connectivity (Roads & Bridges), Rs 555.80 crores for Industries and Commerce (an augmentation of Rs 139.84 crores from the previous year's allocation), Rs 198.07 crores for Social Security Expenditures, and Rs 312.57 crores for Youth Empowerment Initiatives, among other sectors.[117]

In the fiscal year of 2023-24, the budget presented in the parliament on 13 March 2023 by Union Finance Minister Nirmala Sitharaman reiterated the Central Government's commitment to further consolidation of good governance in the UT. This was needed to usher in accelerated development for inclusive growth by facilitating the inflow of investments and industrial growth and by creating new avenues of employment for the youth of the state. For the fiscal year 2023-24, the total receipts were estimated at Rs 1,18,500 crores. Out of this, Rs 1,06,061 crores constitutes Revenue Receipts, Rs 12,439 crores are Capital Receipts, and Rs 30,000 crores is in the form of Ways & Means Advances. The UT's own revenues, inclusive of both tax and non-tax sources, are projected to be Rs 34,942 crores. Additionally, Rs 35,581 crores is anticipated as Central Assistance and Rs 26,786 crores as Central Sector Schemes/ Prime Minister's Development Package) for the Union Territory of Jammu and Kashmir

(CSS/ PMDP). Given these receipts, the total estimated expenditure for the period is projected at Rs 1,18,500 crores. Within this, capital expenditure is set at Rs 41,491 crores, while revenue expenditure is expected to be Rs 77,009 crores. It further projected a Revenue Surplus of Rs 29,052 crores for the available (for capital expenditure) and a Fiscal Deficit of Rs 12,012 crores.[118]

To bolster J&K's socioeconomic progress, the government allocated substantial capital expenditure across various sectors. A breakdown of these capital expenditure allocations for the fiscal year 2023-24 reveals the following amounts: Rs 2,526.74 crores for Agriculture and Horticulture Sectors (an increase of Rs 1,239.45 crores from the previous year's allocation), Rs 629.70 crores for Animal, Sheep Husbandry, and Fisheries Sectors (an increase of Rs 267.84 crores from the previous year's allocation), Rs 2,097.53 crores for Health and Medical Education Sector (an increase of Rs 214.97 crores from the previous year's allocation), Rs 4,169.26 crores for the Rural Sector, Rs1,964.90 crores for the Power Sector, Rs 457.39 crores for Tourism and Culture Sectors (an increase of Rs 54.31 crores from the previous year's allocation), Rs 2,928.04 crores for Housing and Urban Development Sector (an increase of Rs 674.78 crores from the previous year's allocation), Rs 1,521.87 crores for School and Higher Education Sector (an increase of Rs193.61 crores from the previous year's allocation), Rs 4,062.87 crores for the Road and Bridge Sector (an increase of Rs98.99 crores from the previous year's allocation), Rs 741.79 crores for Industries and Commerce Sector (an increase of Rs 283.40 crores from the previous year's allocation), Rs 98.92 crores for the Social Security Sector, Rs 396.63 crores for Youth Empowerment, Employment, Entrepreneurship, skill Development and Sports Activities, Rs 207.75 crores for the Forest, Ecology and

Environment Sector (an increase of Rs 68.52 crores from the previous year's allocation), Rs 390.87 crores for Food Civil Supplies and Consumer Affairs (an increase of Rs 21.49 crores from the previous year's allocation), and Rs 109.85 crores for Science & Technology (an increase of Rs 37.00 crores from the previous year's allocation), among other sectors.[119]

The budgetary trajectory of J&K since its transition into a Union Territory reflects the region's evolving economic landscape and developmental aspirations. The initial budget adjustments following the reorganisation in 2019 were necessary to accommodate the new administrative structure. Subsequent budgets aimed at enhancing governance, promoting investment and achieving inclusive growth. While the 2020-21 budget showcased optimism in development, subsequent fiscal years witnessed a discrepancy between projected and actual revenues, highlighting economic management challenges. Notably, the emphasis on sectors such as agriculture, health, education and infrastructure in allocating capital expenditure underscores the government's commitment to holistic progress. The government's efforts to enhance transparency, eradicate corruption and implement innovative systems such as BEAMS signify an evolving governance framework. The continuous budgetary emphasis on developmental sectors, coupled with efforts to attract industrial investment and empower local communities, illustrates the long-term vision to transform the Union Territory into a model of prosperity and opportunity.

Developmental Initiatives

Following the de-operationalisation of Article 370 on 5 August 2019, the Union Territory of Jammu and Kashmir witnessed a qualitative shift in its developmental trajectory. There was a renewed governmental emphasis on accelerating the economic growth of the region through the adoption of policies in favour of substantial upgradation of infrastructure and facilitation of investments. Earlier, the successive state governments had shown reticence towards building a business-friendly ecosystem citing various regulatory frameworks that effectively deterred any kind of external investments in the region.

However, in the new political landscape, the UT administration was empowered enough to reverse that scenario. It has proactively removed those obstacles and adopted pro-business measures, including the creation of a 6,000-acre-strong government-owned land bank. This resulted in enhanced confidence among the investors, who showed strong willingness to invest in different sectors of J&K's economy. This is reflected in the J&K government's signing of over 168 Memorandums of Understanding (MoUs) with various companies, collectively amounting to Rs 13,600 crores. The government's attention has thereby been refocused on revitalising the regional economy. As part of this, the Kashmir Valley achieved a significant milestone by securing a foreign direct investment (FDI) infusion of Rs 500 crores for the first time. This FDI, spearheaded by Dubai-based Emaar Enterprises, was for the construction of a multifaceted shopping and office complex.

The UT government also established the Jammu and Kashmir Infrastructure Development Finance Corporation as a special vehicle for providing crucial financial backing to a range of previously dormant projects. While doing so, it adopted a comprehensive approach by shortlisting 14 socio-economic sectors such as tourism, electricity generation, education and healthcare for routing investments to drive the UT's holistic development. This influx of foreign investments underscores J&K's growing appeal as an attractive destination for business and investment opportunities. The infusion of capital into the above shortlisted sectors has the potential to catalyse economic growth further and create employment opportunities for the local population.

Augmenting the road networks, which happen to be among the important drivers of economic development, forms an important part of Prime Minister Narendra Modi's vision for infrastructural advancement of the country. In line with this vision, various pending projects have received official approval, with simultaneous efforts aimed at overcoming obstacles hindering ongoing projects being made. An illustrative example of this accelerated project execution is the Rambagh–Jehangir Chowk flyover in Srinagar. Interestingly, the completion of this mere 2.4-km-long flyover project had dragged on for nearly a decade, as against the initial three-year deadline of 2016 when the work was initiated in 2013, due to local administrative hurdles. As a testament to the pronounced sense of developmental urgency, the allocation of resources under the Prime Minister's Development Programme for the UT doubled from 27 per cent to 54 per cent.

The enhanced impetus to improve the road infrastructure in the region is also signified by the near-completion of the four-lane Srinagar–Jammu National Highway project, which has significantly reduced travel time between the two capital cities of the UT. A number of tunnels such as the 8.5-kilometre-long Qazigund-Banihal tunnel and 9.28-kilometre-long Chenani-Nashri tunnel, India's longest road tunnel, have been made operational during this period, which has smoothened the travel experience on this highway. Cumulatively, road infrastructure projects aimed at last-mile connectivity and valued at Rs 5,979 crores have received the requisite sanction, with 506 such projects having already achieved successful completion. This includes projects such as the Jammu-Akhnoor Road, Chenani-Sudhmahadev Road, Jammu-Udhampur Road, Jammu Ring Road, Srinagar Ring Road and Kangan-Kargil Road. This increased pace of road infrastructure improvement in J&K is demonstrated by its achievement of the construction of 3,300 kilometres of rural roads during 2020-21 alone, as revealed by the UT government in 2021.

The long wait for Kashmir to join the nationwide rail network is finally over, with the successful trials over the Srinagar–Jammu railway track in January 2024 and a formal inauguration scheduled for July 2024. In completing this track, the Indian engineers have accomplished an engineering marvel by constructing the world's highest railway bridge over the Chenab River, notwithstanding the topographic and geological challenges in the terrain. This towering bridge, constructed at an elevation of 359 metres above sea level, boasts a central span measuring an imposing 467 metres, symbolising an unwavering commitment to infrastructural advancement on a grand scale. The construction of this bridge formed the single largest challenge in realising the dream of connecting Kashmir Valley with the Indian mainland, a project that was conceived in the early 1980s.

Likewise, in light of the government's commitment to rejuvenate dormant developmental initiatives and invigorate the broader economic landscape, the infrastructural refurbishment in the electricity generation sector has also witnessed a qualitative push with liberal capital spending by the government. For instance, hydro projects like Ujh, Shahpur Kandi and Ganderbal, which languished in a state of stasis for more than half a century, have seen a change of fortunes with the work commencing and gradually taking pace.

This developmental push is also demonstrated in the ongoing twin smart city projects of Srinagar and Jammu, which are being implemented to rejuvenate the urban infrastructure in the UT. Under this, the government is undertaking 309 projects worth 4000 crores in both these cities, of which 187 projects have been completed as of December 2023, as revealed by the Union Ministry of Housing and Urban Affairs.

Apart from encouraging and facilitating outside investments into the UT, the local government, with support from the Central Government, has undertaken ambitious structural reforms to streamline administrative processes towards fostering a conducive environment for entrepreneurial pursuits. Within this framework, the education sector has gained increased significance with dozens of new colleges, both technical and conventional, established in the UT. For instance, seven new medical colleges have been established since 2019 and have already started functioning, taking the number of medical education seats to over 1200 from a mere 485 in 2018. J&K has also received sanction for two national-level medical institutes—All India Institute of Medical Sciences (AIIMS) Jammu (in Vijaypur) and AIIMS Kashmir (in Awantipora)—under the government's comprehensive healthcare infrastructure development plans for the region.

J&K's Development Driven Policy Transformation

The UT government has adopted several policies to drive this growth and streamline the governance-related procedures to facilitate the entry of developmental actors and partners. Noteworthy among these policy documents are the Jammu and Kashmir Industrial Policy 2021, New Central Sector Scheme 2021, Jammu and Kashmir IT/ITES Policy 2020, Jammu and Kashmir Wool Processing, Handloom, Handicrafts Policy 2020, Jammu and Kashmir Affordable

Housing, Slum Redevelopment and Rehabilitation, and Township Policy 2020, Jammu and Kashmir Poultry Policy 2020, Jammu and Kashmir Industrial Land Allotment Policy 2021 and Jammu and Kashmir Film Policy 2021, all released by the UT government. The following is a brief overview of these policies. These interventions have resulted in enhanced confidence among the investors, who showed willingness to route their investments in different sectors of J&K's economy.

A. The Jammu and Kashmir Industrial Policy 2021: Driving UT's Industrial Growth

For seven decades, J&K saw limited expansion of industries, with the result that the industrial imprint on the landscape of the region was very limited. Successive local governments failed to establish any credible industrial base in J&K, making it overwhelmingly dependent on the outside world for everything possible. To break this cycle of stagnancy, the UT government has introduced a series of robust initiatives, including implementing various policy measures to attract external investments towards stimulating economic growth and industrial development in the region.

Among these measures, the government adopted the Jammu and Kashmir Industrial Policy 2021 on 19 April 2021. With the slogan of 'Tradition, Growth and Transformation', the policy sought to transform J&K from an 'aspirational' to an 'industrialised' region. It was retrospectively implemented from 1 April 2021, with the government emphasising the provision of 'a regulatory environment within a supportive framework of Ease of Doing business'. As per the government, this was meant to' 'address the challenges" faced by the industrial sector of J&K and create a "Sustainable, Balanced, Progressive and Competitive ecosystem" in the Union Territory. "It aimed to initiate the industrialisation process at the grassroots level by utilising local resources, skills and domestic talents. The policy explicitly pledged an era of vast socioeconomic advancement within J&K that catered to the needs and desires of its people, while also removing the bottlenecks for external investors to set up their ventures in the region. As such, the policy objective outlined that it will create:

> ... a conducive ecosystem for industry, which attracts investments in focus sectors leading to sustainable, equitable, environment friendly and balanced industrial development thereby creating employment opportunities for the youth, income generation and overall development of the region.[120]

Under this policy, the UT outlined its focus areas of development, which include manufacturing, IT/ITES, agriculture and food processing, healthcare and pharmaceuticals, infrastructure and real estate, herbal and medicinal plants, milk, poultry and wool production, education and skill development, tourism and hospitality, film tourism, horticulture and post-harvest management, renewable energy, handloom and handicrafts as well as export-oriented units.

The policy offered a comprehensive range of benefits for existing industrial enterprises and potential investors. As per this policy, all industrial units that commenced commercial production from 1 April, as well as the units undergoing substantial expansion at that time, were eligible for incentives. Meanwhile, the existing units that qualified for incentives under the previous Industrial Policy of 2016 could continue to avail of these benefits until 31 March 2026. In terms of incentives, it offered exemption of stamp duty and court fee for new and existing units undertaking expansion, subsidy on procurement of quality certificates, automation, pollution control devices, green and environment protection initiatives, turnover incentives and SGST incentive, apart from providing marketing support and other benefits.[121]

This new policy differs from all the industrial policies that were previously in effect. The past administrations of the former J&K state had adopted various industrial policies over time (such as in 1995, 1998 and 2004), with the most recent being the Industrial Policy of 2016. The Central Government introduced incentive packages to support these earlier industrial policies at different intervals, including the Central Capital Investment Scheme of 2002 and 2012, the Scheme of Budgetary Support under the Goods and Services Tax regime and JKIDS 2018. Despite these efforts, the industrial sector in the Kashmir region struggled to compete with other parts of the country.

The Central Government supplemented the J&K Industrial Policy 2021 with the New Central Sector Scheme 2021 of the Union Ministry of Commerce, which was announced on 19 February 2021. The scheme has the objective of transforming the industrial ecosystem of J&K, has a financial outlay of over Rs 28,400 crores and will remain in force for 16 years from 2021-22 to 2036-37.[122] The incentives under this scheme include Capital Investment Incentive (CII), Capital Interest Subvention (CIS), Goods & Services Tax Linked Incentive (GSTLI) and Working Capital Interest Subvention (WCIS).[123] Additionally, the J&K UT government also approved an economic revitalisation plan of Rs 1,352.99 crores in September 2020.[124]

Another policy intervention to supplement the Industrial Policy is the Jammu and Kashmir Industrial Land Allotment Policy 2021-30. The J&K government approved it on 22 January 2021 with the objective of "evolving a fair and transparent mechanism for land allotment for industrial use" in order to "achieve inclusive growth and bring economic prosperity through sustainable industrialisation and employment generation" across the length and breadth of the Union Territory.[125] It seeks to convert industrially viable land into a well-organised industrial land bank to encourage balanced industrial expansion within the Union Territory.

While removing the obstacles related to land acquisition that for long hindered the industrial progress of the region, the policy framework outlined that the land will be readily accessible for allocation to legitimate entrepreneurs, initially for a period of 40 years, and on extension, for up to 99 years. The goal is to shift the region from being land-restricted to becoming an attractive destination for industrial investment, aligning with national policies.[126] As such, the UT government was able to establish a 6,000-acre strong land bank to facilitate the land allotment for interested parties to help expand their industrial imprint in the region. Notably, this effort involved the transfer of land parcels totalling 2,125 acres in the Jammu region, and an additional 1,000 acres in the Kashmir region, to the Department of Industries and Commerce, accounting for more than 50 per cent of the designated land.

The Land Allotment Policy further proposed dividing industrial areas into zones at both block and municipality levels, considering factors such as the current industrial activity in the region, its geographical location and the degree of urbanisation.[127] Consequently, the UT administration identified and officially recognised 292 industrial zones spread across various districts within the UT under the Allotment Policy of 2021-30, which provided guidelines for land allocation for such enterprises. The government constituted a high-level committee to administer the land allotment process, with the direction to adhere to a specified timeline, ensuring a review period of thirty days, which was extended to forty-five days for projects involving an investment of Rs 200 crores or more. This ensured that the allotment was undertaken on a fast-track basis to remove the systemic hurdles. As such, investors were granted land under a lease agreement, with an initial term of 40 years, with the provision for extension up to 99 years.

This intervention through the New Industrial Policy 2021 yielded significant results for the industrial prosperity of the region, transforming it into an investment destination. By April 2021, the J&K government had signed 456 memoranda of understanding (MOUs) with companies, securing investment commitments worth Rs 23,152 crores.[128] Additionally, the J&K held its first-ever Real Estate Summit at Jammu on 27 December 2021, during which the UT Government signed another 39 Memorandum of Understandings (MoUs) "worth Rs 18,300 crores with the country's real estate investors for the development of housing and commercial projects with the country's largest realtors."[129]

Of particular mention here is the significant interest demonstrated by over 40 major Indian business conglomerates, including globally renowned Tata and Reliance groups, in investing in J&K. These businesses showcased a diverse range of investment inclinations, encompassing infrastructure development, horticulture, renewable energy, tourism, information technology, defence and renewable energy initiatives. The government-owned land bank has assumed major significance in this regard, as the allotment of land resources to the investing companies to establish their units got smoothened. This constitutes a landmark transition for the region, facilitated in full by the removal of Article 35A. This earlier acted as a major impediment for the non-local investors from making such forays in the region, as it disallowed them from purchasing or owning land resources in J&K. This, in particular, afforded private sector entities the opportunity to participate in the real estate and hospitality sector of the UT and help refurbish the infrastructural needs of J&K as the volume of economic activities in such sectors expanded.

As such, the UT received yet its "highest-ever" investments of Rs 1,547.87 crores in 2022-23. This was revealed by the Union Minister of State for Home, Government of India, Nityanand Rai, during parliamentary proceedings on 14 March 2023.[130] J&K achieved a significant milestone in its recent history with the first successful investment by the UAE-based Emaar group. The group launched a mega mall project worth Rs 250 crores, the biggest in the UT, with 500 shops in Srinagar in March 2023. The multinational group further committed an investment of Rs 250 crores to set up IT towers in the UT's capital city.[131]

In terms of local employment generation through these interventions, government data reveals that the newly operational businesses in the fiscal year 2022-23 created over 10,000 job opportunities in the Union Territory. These figures were expected to jump further during the 2023-24 fiscal year, as new industrial projects worth Rs 5500 crores started functioning in J&K.[132] Nevertheless, if the figures of the J&K Industries Department, which is the official implementing agency of the Industrial Policy, are any indication, the UT is poised to receive investments worth over Rs 66,000 crores in the coming years through over 5,327 proposals received by the government.

Therefore, it can be argued that the Industrial Policy of 2021 established a comprehensive framework for the overall industrial development of J&K. As such, as revealed by the investment inflow to the region following its adoption, the policy marked a significant stride towards transforming J&K

into an industrially advanced region. These local efforts to redress industrial challenges were ably supplemented by the Central Government's handholding, which has liberally infused the UT with required capital under initiatives such as the New Central Sector Scheme of 2021.

This has gradually changed the narrative about J&K from one of an unfavourable business/industrial ecosystem to that of a friendly landscape, giving a ray of hope for fostering sustainability, progress and competition in the Union Territory. By promoting grassroots industrialisation using local resources and skills, these measures have the potential to drive the socio-economic growth of J&K by generating employment opportunities for the locals, provided that the governments in Srinagar and New Delhi continue sustaining an investment-friendly climate in the UT.

B. Building Sustainable Real Estate in J&K

Real-estate investments, like other sectors, despite their high potential, evaded J&K for a long. When the government of India adopted the Real Estate (Regulation & Development) Act (RERA), 2016, it was described as one of the liberal central laws for making the interests of people supreme, to regulate the sector and secure the interests of people and businesses alike by establishing "an adjudicating mechanism for speedy dispute redressal". However, the law could not be applied to J&K on account of limitations placed under Article 370.

As such, within a year of the implementation of the Jammu and Kashmir Re-Organisation Act 2019, the Central Government extended the jurisdiction of RERA to J&K in October 2020, stimulating real estate development initiatives in the region and facilitating its swift expansion.

As mandated by the Act, the J&K government also constituted RERA in February 2021 to oversee the expansion and development of the real estate sector in the region and enable investors from outside the UT, who for long were constrained from making any foray into the market and contributing to its development.

Additionally, the UT administration adopted many other significant 'initiatives including full digital processing of all files, digitisation of land records and deemed approval for change of land use (CLU) after 30 days of filing applications' to transform the sector. Land resources, which previously remained out of the hands of investors, was made readily available by the government, which even incentivised investments in the sector. For instance, in the capital city of Srinagar, the UT government made 700 acres of land available "for integrated residential development',' along with "another 200 acres on Srinagar Ring Road for high-end residential development',' as was revealed by the Housing & Urban Development Department in December 2021.[133]

These interventions in the real estate sector are significant, given the increased housing demands spurred by growing urbanisation in the cities of Srinagar and Jammu, even as J&K maintained relatively favourable housing conditions compared to other states. Nevertheless, there was a discernible need for housing investments, particularly to accommodate first-time homebuyers within the Union Territory.

C. **Revitalising Tourism Sector: Jammu and Kashmir Tourism Policy 2020**

Jammu and Kashmir maintains a distinct position on India's tourism map, with increased visibility on the global stage. The diverse offerings in J&K include sport, adventure, medical and religious tourism.

As a prominent tourist destination, the region's natural beauty offers diverse attractions including forests, lakes, mesmerising backwaters, hill stations and landscapes, making for a captivating and hospitable environment. The region boasts of historical monuments, religious sites and more, drawing visitors from across the world. The region's rich composite religio-cultural milieu, having significant populations from major faiths living side by side, also offers distinct avenue for pilgrimage tourism with famous pilgrimage sites such as Shri Amarnathji shrine, Mata Vaishno Devi shrine and Baba Ghulam Shah Badshah shrine, among others, attracting numerous devotees. The state's historical forts, museums and heritage sites help preserve its history and contribute to its everlasting appeal.[134] There is also significant potential for medical tourism due to its pleasant and pollution-free climate, tradition of indigenous medicine and upcoming healthcare facilities such as the two AIIMSs mentioned earlier. The flourishing tourism sector contributes substantially to the state's economy and employment, offering a wide range of job opportunities ranging from hotel managers to tour guides and photographers.

Following J&K's constitutional realignment within the Union of India, the UT has undergone a remarkable cross-sectoral transformation with improved security dynamics. It marks the gradual emergence of J&K from the three-decade-long tumultuous period of Pakistan-sponsored terrorism, during which time tourism suffered greatly because of heightened insecurity among both locals and visitors, like other sectors. This change is demonstrated by reduced terror incidents and an end to the sponsored stone-pelting phenomenon that headlined the last three decades, especially during the 2010-2019 period. For instance, as compared to 1,488 stone-pelting incidents in 2018 and 1,999 incidents in 2019, J&K recorded no such incidents in 2021.

This security transformation has changed the narrative

around J&K beyond the headlines to that of a lead tourist destination in the country with an actual surge in the number of both domestic and international tourist arrivals. For instance, even as the world reeled from the aftermath of the COVID-19 global pandemic in 2022, J&K recorded an unprecedented surge in the number of tourist arrivals. The UT government revealed that J&K welcomed 18.8 million tourists in 2022, which surpassed 20.2 million in 2023, the highest-ever figure since independence. This also included over 50 thousand foreign tourists in 2023, signifying Kashmir's return to the itineraries of foreign tourists as one of the major attractions in India.[135] This influx of tourists not only bolstered the region's economy, but also fostered better understanding normalised situation in Kashmir on the one hand and improved awareness about the ground reality in Kashmir in rest of India on the other. (see Table 5.5).

Table 5.5 Number of tourist arrivals in J&K

Year	DTVs*	FTVs**
2010	99,73,189	48,099
2011	1,30,71,531	71,593
2012	1,24,27,122	78,802
2013	1,08,91,424	60,845
2014	94,38,544	86,477
2015	1,33,12,754	56,153
2016	1,26,61,174	53,985
2017	1,45,46,738	33,253
2018	1,68,78,025	90,043
2019	1,61,63,330	57,920
2020	25,19,524	5,317
2021	1,13,14,920	1,650
2022	1,88,84,317	19,985

Data Source: Department of Tourism, UT Government of J&K * DTVs: Domestic Tourist Visits ** FTVs: Foreigner Tourist Visits

Given the importance of this sector to the local economy, the newfound stability and security prompted the UT Government to launch various initiatives to refurbish the tourism infrastructure in the region with the aim of smoothening the leisure experience of tourists. Towards this end, the government adopted the Jammu and Kashmir Tourism Policy 2020 on 18 March 2020, setting an ambitious goal to attract Rs 20 billion in investments during the 2020-25 period. It set forth a "dynamic long-term" vision to fully tap into the growth prospects of Jammu & Kashmir's tourism sector and position the Union Territory as the premier year-round tourist destination "that is natural in its environment, global in standards, modern in outlook, traditional in hospitality, entertaining in experience and thrilling in adventure". It concurrently envisages creating sustainable livelihood prospects for the local populace. In this pursuit, the policy puts forth a series of proactive measures, enticing incentives and imperative regulatory adjustments to foster substantial investment through efficient administration and private partnerships.[136]

The policy also intends to provide training to approximately 4,000 tourist service providers within the next decade. It seeks to endorse diverse forms of tourism such as Adventure Tourism, Horti-Tourism, Saffron Tourism, Angling/Game Fishing, Cultural Tourism, Eco Circuit Tourism, Film Tourism, Golf Tourism, Heritage Tourism, MICE (Meetings, Incentives, Conferences & Exhibition) Tourism, Religious / Spiritual Tourism, Wellness Tourism, and Rural/ Village Tourism across the Union Territory.

Driven by this policy initiative, the UT government has taken various measures to invigorate the tourism sector. Notably, considering its commitment to expanding tourism, the government has approved seven new trekking routes for development in wildlife-protected areas to boost ecotourism. Further, the commencement of late evening flights to and from Srinagar International Airport demonstrates the government's seriousness in ensuring hassle-free connectivity to the region. Further, in another significant initiative, the UT government launched the "Jammu and Kashmir Tourist Village Network" under the "Mission Youth" programme. This seeks to convert 75 historically significant, picturesque and culturally rich villages into tourist destinations.[137]

Besides, as part of this endeavour, the J&K government introduced a rural homestay project in 2022 with the objective of immersing tourists in local culture, cuisine and traditions. It offered special financial incentives, providing Rs 50,000 in assistance for each homestay unit. By December 2022, this initiative had resulted in the establishment of over 200 homestays, enabling domestic and international tourists to engage with the region's rural heritage while experiencing local hospitality.

The UT Government also collaborated with hospitality tech company OYO, which resulted in the 'Crown of Incredible India' rural tourism initiative. This aims to rejuvenate the tourism industry and empower the youth in J&K to become startup entrepreneurs.[138] It also intends to encourage sustainable tourism led by young individuals, community entrepreneurship and women's empowerment through employment opportunities. The scheme provides various benefits, including up to Rs 10 lakh for infrastructure, camping equipment, homestays and financial support for filming projects by empanelled companies and local groups. These efforts collectively aim to boost the rural economy and the tourism sector.

The above efforts not only enhance economic prospects but also promise to bolster the local employment landscape.

These have elevated the tourism sector to the level of a crucial component of the UT's economic landscape by generating substantial annual revenues amounting to Rs 80 billion, thereby elevating its share to a record 7-8 per cent in J&K's GDP. This is particularly significant, given that the sector serves as a vital source of direct and indirect employment, providing livelihood opportunities to approximately 100,000 individuals within J&K.

One of the biggest campaigns to refocus the conversation about Kashmir as one of the most prominent tourism destinations globally was strategically conducted by the Government of India, under its presidency as the Chair of G20, the economic group of the world's twenty major economies, through its decision to host the 3rd G20 Tourism Working Group Meeting in Srinagar from 22-24 May 2023. The event brought over 60 delegates from major world economies to the UT capital, not only testifying about the return of normalcy in the region but also extending an invitation to the world to visit and explore what has been referred to as the 'paradise on earth'.[139]

In summary, the post-2019 period has marked a significant transformation in the Kashmir Valley, resulting in its revitalisation as a vibrant tourist hotspot. This transformation has not only stimulated economic development, but has also heralded a redefined security environment, enabling the implementation of initiatives aimed at enriching the tourist experience and attracting foreign investments. These advancements carry substantial potential for the ongoing prosperity and integration of Jammu and Kashmir into both the national and international arenas.

D. Jammu and Kashmir Film Policy 2021

Closely aligned with the government's push for rejuvenating the tourism industry of J&K is the adoption of the Jammu and Kashmir Film Policy 2021. The UT's Administrative Council approved it on 5 August 2021. The Indian Film Industry has a long association with the region dating back to the 1960s, when Kashmir's breathtaking landscape captivated the imagination of Bollywood directors, thereby making it to the celluloid screens of the country and beyond. The scenic beauty of the region makes it a cinematographer's dream. Films such as *Kashmir Ki Kali, Jab Jab Phool Khile, Himalaya Ki God Mein* and *Janwar* brought the region's scenic landscape into people's eyes worldwide.

Despite a hiatus due to external turmoil due to Pakistan-sponsored militancy, which dissuaded the filmmakers for a while, the region regained the attention of the filmmakers, with iconic movies such as *Mission Kashmir, Laila Majnu, Shikara, Jab Tak Hai Jaan, Bajrangi Bhaijaan* and *Rockstar* being filmed in the Valley. Movies like *Laila Majnu, Shikara* and *Haider* amplified local narratives on the silver screen.

Acknowledging the cinematic potential of the Union Territory, the 2021 Film Policy aspires to position Jammu & Kashmir as the primary choice for filmmakers seeking shooting locations. At its core is the ambition to make the UT a favoured film shooting destination, backed by appealing incentives. This initiative not only envisions generating employment within the UT, but also aims to attract heightened investment to the local film industry. A key objective is the creation of all-weather filming locations.

To materialise these ambitions, the J&K Film Policy proposed the establishment of the Jammu & Kashmir Film Development Council (JKFDC). It is expected to operate as an independent entity, serving to realise the objectives of the policy effectively. Furthermore, it proposes the formation of a J&K Film Division "for showing the short/educational films made in J&K in the cinema houses'.[140]

A significant advancement within the policy is the designation of the Film Sector as an Industry in J&K. The policy introduces a comprehensive array of subsidies, ranging from a subsidy of up to Rs 1 crore for a first film to a subsidy of up to Rs 5 crores for a film based on a J&K-specific theme. A brief overview of these incentives is listed below:

1. For the first film, a subsidy of up to Rs 1 crore or 25 per cent of the COP, whichever is lower, is offered if at least 50 per cent of the total shooting days take place in the UT. Likewise, a subsidy of up to Rs 1.50 crores or 25 per cent of the total COP, whichever is lower, is provided if a minimum of 75 per cent of total shooting days is in the UT.
2. For the second film, subsidies are set at up to Rs 1.25 crore or 25 per cent of the total COP, whichever is lower, if a minimum of 50 per cent of total shooting days occur in the UT. Similarly, it increases to up to Rs 1.75 crore or 25 per cent of the total COP, whichever is lower, for a minimum of 75 per cent of total shooting days in the UT.
3. For the third film, subsidies range up to Rs 1.50 crore or 25 per cent of the total COP, whichever is lower, if a minimum of 50 per cent of total shooting days are spent in the UT. Likewise, it extends to up to Rs 2.00 crores or 25 per cent of the total COP, whichever is lower, for a minimum of 75 per cent of total shooting days in the UT.
4. For a film based on a story or script centred around the UT of J&K, known as a J&K-Specific Film, the filmmaker will be entitled to a special grant of 50 per cent of the film's COP or Rs 5.00 crores, whichever is less.[141]

The policy introduces a separate subsidy provision for films produced by nationally or internationally acclaimed directors or producers who have previously received subsidies for films made in the UT. The maximum subsidy amount varies from Rs 1.75 crores to Rs 3.25 crores based on whether it's for the second, third or subsequent films in the UT. Additionally, the policy outlines detailed subsidy provisions for various types of productions such as films, TV shows, web series, original content on OTT platforms and documentary films intended to be shot in Jammu & Kashmir. In this context, the maximum permissible subsidy for permission fees is up to Rs 1 crore.[142]

The rationale behind offering these substantial subsidies is that when a feature film extensively features J&K with over 75 per cent of shooting days in the UT, it directly benefits the local tourism sector. While film portrayal can lead to an immediate increase in tourist activity, visitor decisions are also influenced by the region's perceived political circumstances at the time of planning a trip to Jammu and Kashmir.

This policy has yielded tangible results, with Lieutenant Governor Manoj Sinha in August 2023 acknowledging the return of J&K as a favoured filming destination. The surge in the number of films and web series shot in the UT, surpassing 300 over a two-year period since introducing the Film Policy in 2021, reflects its successful impact, ushering in a new era of peace and development. As per Sinha, 'J&K is regaining its status as a preferred film location. The era of the 1980s, marked by Hollywood and Bollywood productions in Kashmir, is making a comeback.'[143]

This exemplifies the tangible positive impact of the policy intervention in successfully rekindling the interest of filmmakers in the region. In conclusion, the Jammu and Kashmir Film Policy 2021 serves as a pivotal step in the government's strategy to revitalise the tourism industry in the region.

E. **Revenue Boom in the Mining Industry**

Parallel to infrastructural overhaul and expansion, the UT

government opened up the mineral mining sector of J&K by making necessary amendments and adjustments in its mining policy, immediately after the de-operationalisation of Article 370 in 2019. In an executive order on 19 March 2019, the J&K government amended provisions of the Jammu and Kashmir Minor Mineral Concession, Storage, Transportation of Minerals and Prevention of Illegal Mining Rules, 2016 to adopt e-auctioning of the mineral blocs instead of its prevalent practice of open auctioning. This is one of the most significant interventions in streamlining the management of J&K's minor minerals such as sand, gravel, boulders, clay, limestone and gypsum and their distribution within and beyond J&K.

This policy intervention allowed more private actors to take part in the sector, including from outside the state. The competition brought more capital revenue for the government, helped increase the UT's locally generated receipts and ensured more resources for its developmental expenditure. Through this formalised and transparent process of auctioning mineral blocs, which for the first time witnessed significant participation from non-local contractors, the J&K government awarded time-bound extraction licenses for 400 small plots in December 2019.

In contrast to the notion that awarding extraction licenses to non-local contracting firms ate away jobs and put the local actors out of work, this process increased the interaction between these actors, which resulted in non-local firms taking the local firms on board by subcontracting their blocs to local miners. Notwithstanding this increased interaction between local and non-local firms, there have been concerns that this increased competition in the sector was inadvertently putting pressure on the common people by increasing the prices of construction materials, including stones, sand, gravel and bricks.

F. Jammu and Kashmir IT/ITES Policy 2020

The Union Territory Government approved the Jammu and Kashmir IT/ITES policy 2020 on 18 March 2020, with the express aim of developing a modern and vibrant ecosystem of Information Technology in the region.[144]

The policy outlined a framework for developing and improving IT infrastructure to cater to both the current and the future e-governance requirements of the Union Territory. It was focused on enhancing digital literacy among the youth to improve their job prospects, attracting investments to the sector, leveraging emerging technologies, encouraging entrepreneurial ventures, generating employment opportunities and ensuring a safer cyberspace for all residents. Its mission statement emphasised the necessity of 'leveraging and harnessing the power of IT…for ensuring a better quality of life for citizens.'[145]

The J&K IT/ITES Policy was designed to streamline approval processes and provide a one-stop clearance system for potential investors. Additionally, the policy introduced an array of financial and non-financial incentives to entice investors. The policy also extended benefits to startups and promoted the establishment of a cutting-edge infrastructure tailored to the needs of the IT/ITES industry.[146]

Through the implementation of this policy, the region aspires to position itself as an attractive hub for the IT industry, fostering investment within the IT/ITES sector. Its vision revolves around harnessing IT as a catalyst for swift, comprehensive and sustainable economic growth in J&K, facilitated by the active involvement of private enterprises.[147]

Regarding the development of infrastructure to attract investments in this field, the policy underscored the government's commitment to creating cutting-edge international-standard infrastructure that aligns with the needs of the IT/ITES industry.

Mega IT hub will be developed, through an initial effort of developing an IT township with a built-up space of 2 million square feet. A signature tower of 1 million square feet shall form the nucleus of the Mega IT hub.[148]

The policy further envisioned the development of integrated townships and IT parks, supplementing the IT Hub's infrastructure, including residential, commercial, and retail spaces, supported by essential amenities such as power, water, sewage systems and street lighting.

To demonstrate its commitment towards implementing the IT Policy and leveraging this sector to provide the necessary technological infrastructure to the local entrepreneurs, the UT administration announced in July 2020 the development of two IT parks in the capital cities of Srinagar and Jammu. With an area of 5 lakh square feet, these parks were meant to encompass IT towers, BPO facilities, expanded infrastructure and housing accommodations for the workforce.[149] The policy document revealed that the government would develop these parks in a cluster mode, wherein "Dedicated/uninterrupted and secure technological infrastructure like optic fibre connectivity, Broad band connectivity, Wi-Fi access, Video Conferencing facilities" will be provided for by the administration.[150]

The policy provided a range of incentives to attract investors from both inside and outside the region. It included a provision for reimbursing up to 25 per cent of lease/rental costs, capped at a maximum of Rs 10 lakh per year for five years, as a way to encourage investment. It reiterated that at least 15 per cent of "plug and play" premises in designated IT parks will be reserved for women entrepreneurs.[151]

G. Jammu and Kashmir Wool Processing, Handloom, Handicrafts Policy 2020

J&K possesses a competitive edge in crafting high-quality fabrics renowned both nationally and internationally, encompassing items such as pashmina and Kani shawls and silk, woollen and cotton textiles among others. The handmade creations from J&K have gained global acclaim due to their exceptional design, artistry and functional significance in generating foreign earnings to fulfil the requirements of the nation and the state. The handicraft sector has notably enriched the industrial framework of the state, with handmade products emerging as a particularly dynamic segment of the economy in recent times. Official records indicate that approximately 378,000 individuals are employed in various forms of handicraft endeavours. In terms of production, this sector occupies a prominent role within the state's industrial landscape.

In recognition of these dynamics and the challenges encountered by these industries, the J&K Government ratified the Jammu and Kashmir Wool Processing, Handloom, Handicrafts Policy 2020 on 27 February 2020. This policy endeavoured to chart a course for the sustainable advancement of the wool, silk, handloom and handicraft sectors in Jammu and Kashmir. It acknowledged the immense potential of these sectors for growth, export, wealth generation and job creation. As such, the policy provided a viable and comprehensive framework for building "a robust eco-system to develop wool processing, handloom and handicrafts sectors" in the Union Territory:

> Jammu and Kashmir will adopt a Cluster-based approach in collaboration with allied Central Government departments to promote the handlooms and handicrafts sector. This shall help to connect backward (raw material banks) and forward linkages (marketing support) as well as easy access

to credit through financial institutions to make the wool, handloom and handicrafts sector vibrant. Skill upgradation through established training institutes like Craft Design Institute, Indian Institute of Carpet Technology and Indian Institute of Handloom Technology will vastly improve the quality of handloom and handicrafts products and help in diversification of the traditional sector and scaling up exports.[152]

The government committed to establishing raw materials banks "to make abundant quantity of certified and graded raw material available to the weavers and artisans" of the region. It further revealed that it intends to declare J&K a Special Economic Zone (SEZ) for wool and silk processing and the handlooms and handicrafts sector, which will bring largescale benefits to the locals including tax holidays and additional incentives. In terms of the financial incentives available to these sectors, the policy emphasised that under the Artisan Credit Scheme, the existing loan amount will be increased from "Rs 1 lakh to Rs 2 lakh with interest subvention of 10 % for a period of 5 years'."[153] Further, all the eligible units engaged in producing and marketing local handicraft products in J&K were expected to receive a one-time working capital subsidy of 10 per cent of their working capital for a year, with a maximum limit of Rs 5.00 lakh. Additionally, these units were also to be granted export subsidies equivalent to 10 per cent of the overall volume of their handicraft products.

One of the significant aspects of the policy is the UT government's express commitment to bringing these industrial sectors within the broader scope of the 'Make in India' programme of the Government of India. This programme offers opportunities for increased investment and improved marketing for handloom and handicraft products.

Conclusion

In conclusion, the events that followed the revocation of Article 370 in August 2019 have significantly transformed the landscape of J&K's integration with the Indian Union. The comprehensive reforms undertaken by the Government of India have addressed deep-rooted issues, paving the way for socioeconomic progress, eradication of large-scale governmental as well as broader political corruption and rectification of historical inequalities. The results of this transformative journey are evident in improved socioeconomic indicators, the empowerment of the local population, the removal of discriminatory laws and the fostering of economic growth.

J&K's economic revitalisation is evident through policy measures that attract investments and promote industrial development. Grassroots democracy has been strengthened with empowered local governance bodies, and the tourism sector has witnessed a resurgence, contributing to the region's global appeal. This progress aligns with India's pursuit of sustainable growth and harmonious integration.

Comparative growth analysis indicates that J&K's positive trajectory is outpacing the national average and several northern states. Despite initial disparities, the UT's per capita income gap has narrowed, showcasing significant progress. In conclusion, J&K's transformation signifies a promising path towards economic prosperity and holistic development.

Conclusion
The Saga of Development will Continue

Jammu and Kashmir has come a long way. After being under the yoke of the Dogra feudal rule for a century, the region embraced a popular and representative system in 1951. This was the hallmark of Indian democracy, notwithstanding recurrent periods of uncertainty over the preceding years. The region had a strategic geopolitical location, being sandwiched between Pakistan and China. It also had some degree of internal autonomy, granted constitutionally on a temporary basis, for the better part of the last seven decades. As such, the region managed to receive undivided attention from the successive governments in New Delhi and was often referred to as the 'crown' of the country. This attention was accompanied by liberal financial grants, including special economic packages at regular intervals by almost every Central Government, to help the J&K government meet its developmental requirements and create new infrastructure in the region. However, this generosity appears to have engendered J&K's continued heavy reliance on Central Government allocations to sustain its budgetary requirements.

It is a truism to say that despite generous funding from New Delhi, successive state governments in Srinagar failed to raise the economic status of the state and build the required developmental infrastructure in proportion to the inflow of funds, as reflected in the continued categorisation of J&K as an 'industrially backward state' in the country with a rather inadequate economic and industrial base. In light of this perceived mismatch between the inflow of funds and the anticipated development dividends, this book constitutes an attempt to examine the overarching narrative of the financial dynamics and socio-economic landscape of J&K over various periods. It maps the inflow of grants-in-aid from the Central Government to Jammu and Kashmir from 1947 onwards Central Government and the socio-economic status of the state over the years. It becomes evident how the lackadaisical approach of the local leadership over the years made J&K heavily dependent on support from outside, specifically the Central Government's grants, to sustain its fiscal expenditures.

The overwhelming role of the Central Government in propping up the finances of the state is a constant in every decade examined in this book, with the share of central grants in J&K's Annual Revenue Receipts being above 50 per cent all along. This was true even during the period from 1947 to the late 1980s, when the state experienced a comparative degree of peace, before Pakistan-sponsored terrorism created major internal security challenges starting from 1989. The state claimed fiscal autonomy under Article 370, which allowed it control over its financial resources. Notwithstanding this, as several data sources reveal, the Central Government continued to support the state with multiple special financial packages in recognition of its distinct geopolitical realities, which elevated its strategic significance to a higher degree. Yet these resources failed to facilitate economic development and modernisation in the 1950s and 1960s to the desired levels, even if a degree of development was achieved in raising basic infrastructure and in the promotion of Kashmir as a prime tourism destination in India. The comparative data from some major states of India during this period suggest that J&K received proportionally higher allocations from the centre. This meant that it was treated with great deal of seriousness and care, perhaps deserving of a border state with a special history of accession to the Union of India.

J&K underwent a prolonged period of tumult. after Pakistan-sponsored terrorism broke out, derailing the governance in the state, necessitating the use of the majority of resources to restore law and order and pushing the issue of development aside for a long while. This externally funded insurgency had profound consequences on the socio-economic and political landscape of the state, including damage to infrastructure and a substantial decline in the tourism sector, which had gradually emerged as an important sector of the economy.

Despite these challenges, concerted efforts led by both central and state administrations gradually restored normalcy, culminating in successful elections in 1996 and restoration of democratic governance, which cooled the nerves inside Kashmir to a certain extent. Like in the past, the subsequent period also saw enhanced central assistance to bolster the region's economy, and J&K's heavy reliance on such support remained a constant in the economic domain. Economic growth indicators demonstrated resilience, albeit with the imperative of further development and diversification. However, successive elected state governments could not deliver on this front.

With a semblance of order following the 1996 State Assembly elections, which brought Farooq Abdullah back as chief minister, J&K underwent a period of democratic rule even in the backdrop of the chaos unleashed by sponsored terrorism. The regular elections became a feature of this phase, with increased people's participation, making it a referendum of sorts against the externally fomented disruptive political narratives. Even during this period, the role of Central Assistance assumed greater significance. Additional financial packages were sanctioned in favour of J&K by different governments in New Delhi, be it headed by either H. D. Deve Gowda, I. K. Gujral, Atal Behari Vajpayee or Dr Manmohan Singh. After the National Democratic Alliance led by BJP assumed power in 2014, with Narendra Modi as Prime Minister, the saga of developmental allocations continued, as did the efforts by spoilers from across the border seeking to vitiate the atmosphere of the state.

Notwithstanding these generous special financial packages, the successive state governments seemed to have been stuck in some sort of systemic logjam. No major headway, which could signify their meaningful interest in leading J&K towards development, was witnessed. The subsequent years demonstrated that the state faced formidable challenges from the deeply entrenched corruption and nepotism within its political framework and governance structure, which hindered the socio-economic progress of the state and eroded public trust. This was symbolised by the state's political class, sans ideological divide, perpetuating a culture of patronage and favouritism and diverting public funds and resources for personal gain, thereby hindering the development of the state. The fact that the state had a special status provided its political leadership with the luxury of relative insulation from central supervision, direction and oversight. The largely valley-centric approach of the state elite coloured their developmental vision, with the result that border areas with bountiful natural resources and tourism potential were neglected for no rhyme or reason.

With the advent of terrorism and senseless violence, there

was a political stasis that facilitated the rise of a culture of unaccountability in administration and apathy among people. Terrorism thrived in such conditions, and the state leadership – basking in the insular impact of the special status – often participated, unwittingly perhaps, in the sustenance of a terror infrastructure in the state that made cross-border interference look natural and perfectly normal. The way the state leaders operated, granting amnesty to the rogue and criminal elements propagating terror and convincing the Central Government of the necessity to mainstream these elements, would suggest that there was a numbing of the sensibility of the people of the state whereby they tolerated terror as a natural phenomenon and a desirable end-state. This was regarded as a price worth paying to safeguard the separate identity of the Kashmiris and their autonomy. In reality, the autonomy granted by the Constitution was misused by the leaders in J&K to fatten themselves, fill their coffers and befool the masses with rhetorical nonsense that made them believe that the only alternative to autonomy was secession and independence, or even accession to Pakistan.

The culture of apathy and corruption is so rooted in J&K society that even after withdrawal of the special status and four years of rule by the centre, the inertial sense of cynicism and negativity threatens to stage a comeback today. Despite efforts by the government to initiate unprecedented development in the entire region in terms of roads, rail and communication infrastructure, supply of water to every household, enhancement of tourism, sports, agriculture and horticulture, provision of security and clean governance, controlling corruption and implementing reforms, many challenges persist. Dealing with this situation requires sustained collaboration between the state and civil society and strengthening of accountability mechanisms, something that would require concerted efforts from the state and the Central Governments.

In this context, the last chapter of the book details the financial position of J&K in the post-Article 370 era, which was revoked on 5 August 2019 to reshape the relationship between Srinagar and New Delhi and achieve J&K's complete integration with the Union of India. Many in Delhi have likened this era to be 'transformational', as the Central Government has unleashed comprehensive reforms aimed at socioeconomic progress, eradication of corruption and economic revitalisation, alongside the empowerment of local governance through strengthened grassroots democracy and a resurgence in the tourism sector. Comparative growth analysis suggests a positive trajectory for J&K, with narrowing disparities in per capita income, signifying progress towards economic prosperity and holistic development of the region.

Nevertheless, even as the post-Article 370 era is still unfolding in front of us and taking roots, it presents a complex yet hopeful picture of Jammu and Kashmir's journey towards peace, security and development. At the same time, it may be recognised that the removal of systemic impediments, which earlier inhibited central oversight and stymied cross-sectoral investments in the region, has gradually started showing results. This is expected to lead to the revitalisation of J&K's economic base, refurbishment of the infrastructure landscape, promotion of industrial development and reclaiming of its rightful place as the prime tourist destination in India for both domestic and foreign visitors. This transformation, however, emphasises the imperative of sustained efforts, collaboration and transparency to realise J&K's full developmental potential.

The resolve of the Indian State under the present government led by prime minister Narendra Modi to bring normalcy and development to the state has so far paid off. There is clarity in the minds of the people today about the approach of the Central Government towards terrorism and governance in J&K. In the last four years, the people of J&K have benefited from the responsive and responsible administration and the economic development delivered by the government in Srinagar. There is a 360-degree developmental overlay on the ground around the state, which is visible, reassuring and apparently sustainable at the moment. Such action-oriented initiatives disincentivise terrorism, and this is perceptible in J&K today with the depleting number of recruits for terror activities across the state. With the return of stability and normalcy to the region, the emphasis of the youth in Kashmir today is to seek out avenues for education and employment rather than bury their future in militancy and in a trigger-happy culture that was encouraged by forces from across the border. This is not to deny that the efforts from across the border continue, even as the ground situation improves in J&K. The attempts by Pakistan to derail peace and push in spurious narratives in Kashmir continue to present a critical and complex challenge to the planners in J&K, who are dedicated to bring peace and prosperity to the state. There is hope and optimism among the people, nevertheless, that the developmental saga unleashed in the recent years will put an end to the spectre of terror and violence on the one hand, and the culture of political negativism on the other, in future.

Name of the Programme/Scheme	Name of the Implementing Agency in the State	Total fund released by GOI during 2008-09 (Rs. in crore)
Accelerated Rural Water Supply Programme	SGO Secretary Finance, PHE Department	403.73
National Rural Health Mission (NRHM)	State Health Department and other agencies	64.69
Sarva Shiksha Abhiyan	Ujala Society, Education Department	205.32
NREGS	Assistant Commissioners DRDA	105.36
Pradhan Mantri Gram Sadak Yojana (PMGSY)	State Rural Roads Agency	191.36
Integrated Child Development Programme	State Social Welfare Department	37.92
Macro Management of Agriculture Schemes	Agriculture Department	18.30
Rural Housing (IAY)	Assistant Commissioners DRDA	71.29
Local Area Development schemes (MPLADS)	District Development Commissioners	25.00
National e-Governance Action Plan	State Department for e-Governance	17.28
	Total	**1140.25**

(Source: CPMS of CHA's website)

Notes

1. The area of the princely state of Jammu and Kashmir covered about 222,797 square kilometres. This region comprised the three administrative divisions of Jammu, Kashmir, and Ladakh, which incorporated the lands of Poonch, Baltistan, and the Gilgit Agency. For more, see, Chitralekha Zutshi, *Languages of Belonging – Islam, Regional Identity and the Making of Kashmir*, Delhi: Permanent Black, 2003, p. 8.
2. Victoria Schofield, *Kashmir in the Crossfire*, London: I.B. Tauris, 1996, p. 40.
3. Ibid, p. 39.
4. Article IV of the Lahore Treaty in Schofield, *Kashmir in the Crossfire*, p. 55.
5. Navnita Chadha Behera, *State, Identity and Violence: Jammu, Kashmir and Ladakh*, New Delhi: Manohar, 2000, p. 37.
6. Mridu Rai, *Hindu Rulers, Muslim Subjects – Islam, Rights and the History of Kashmir*, Delhi: Permanent Black, 2007, p. 26.
7. Ibid, p. 30.
8. Mohan Krishen Teng, Ram Krishen Kaul Bhatt and Santosh Kaul, *Kashmir: Constitutional History and Documents*, New Delhi: Light and Life Publishers, 1977, p. 16.
9. Ibid, p. 16. See, also Schofield, *Kashmir*, p. 56.
10. Schofield, *Kashmir*, p. 56.

11 Teng *et al.*, *Kashmir: Constitutional History*, p. 17.
12 Ibid, p. 18.
13 Behera, *State, Identity and Violence*, p. 37.
14 Zutshi, *Languages of Belonging–Islam, Regional Identity and the Making of Kashmir*, Delhi: Permanent Black, 2003, p. 58.
15 Teng *et al.*, *Kashmir: Constitutional History*, p. 18.
16 The 'resident' was a colonial official who advised the ruler.
17 Teng *et al.*, *Kashmir: Constitutional History*, p. 36.
18 Different variations of the *nasaq* system were dominant in Berar, Bengal, and Kashmir. For more information, see, Irfan Habib, *The Agrarian System of Mughal India*, 1556-1707, New Delhi: Oxford University Press, 1999, p. 258.
19 Rattan Lal Hangloo, *The State in Medieval Kashmir*, New Delhi: Manohar Publishers, 2000, p. 112.
20 Ibid.
21 Habib's exploration of the agrarian system discusses the method of revenue generation that was prominent in earlier centuries within the state. For more, see, Habib, *The Agrarian System of Mughal India, 1556-1707*, New Delhi: Oxford University Press, 1999, p. 263.
22 Zutshi, *Languages of Belonging*, pp. 70-71.
23 P N K Bamzai, *Socio-Economic History of Kashmir* (1846-1925), New Delhi: Metropolitan, 1988, 1987, p. 124.
24 Land distribution among cultivators was termed *nafre*, where a unit comprised a man, his wife, and a grown-up child. This group received four acres of irrigated land. A *nim nafre* consisted of a man and his wife, while a *pao nafre* referred to a bachelor, each receiving 2 acres and 1.5 acres, respectively. For more, see, Bamzai, *Socio-Economic History*, p. 120.
25 Ibid, p. 118.
26 Zutshi, *Languages of Belonging*, p. 64. Kashmiri weights: 1 *kharwa*r = 80 kgs, 16 *traks* = 1 *kharwar*, 1 *seer* kasmiri = 960

grams; Source: Bamzai, *Socio-Economic History*, p. 133.

27 Shakti Kak (2007) 'The agrarian system of the princely state of Jammu and Kashmir: A study of colonial settlement policies, 1860-1905', in Ernst, Waltraud and Biswamoy Pati, eds. (2007) *India's Princely States: People, Princes and Colonialism*. London: Routledge, p. 73.

28 Throughout its history, Kashmir has seen multiple famines, all mostly brought on by floods. Kashmir saw two devastating famines in the 19th century: one in 1831, when the Sikhs were in power, and in 1865 and 1878, when the Dogra government was in power. But the famine of 1878—the worst by far—shadowed the famine that occurred earlier in 1865, both during the reign of Ranbir Singh. Several agencies have reported that the famine that occurred between 1877 and 1879 claimed a significant number of lives. It is reported that Srinagar's population fell from 127,400 to 60,000, although other people think that just two-fifths of the original population survived. It also took Kashmir more than 20 years to recover from the loss of its economy and labour force (for details see: Shabir Ahmad Sheikh and Irm Jalali Bodha, 'Famine in Kashmir: The Policy of Dogra Ruler: 1846-1925', *International Journal on Arts, Management and Humanities*, Vol. 5, Issue 2, 2016, pp. 26-32).

29 Please see Robert Thorp (1868) *Cashmere Misgovernment: An Account of the Economic and Political Oppression of the People of Cashmere by the Maharaja's Government*. Calcutta: Wyman Bros.

30 Raja Sukh Jiwan Mal, originally from Punjab and Hindu by faith, was born in Kabul, which is why he is referred to as Afghan here.

31 W R Lawrence. *The Valley of Kashmir*. London: Henry Frowde, 1895.

32. A Gani (1990). Industrial Relations in Jammu and Kashmir. *Indian Journal of Agrarian Relations*, 1990, Vol. 26, Issue 1, pp. 53--67.
33. P N K Bamzai, *Socio-Economic History of Kashmir 1846-1925*, New Delhi: Metropolitan, 1988, p.239.
34. Ratan Chand Rawlley, *The Silk Industry and Trade: A Study in the Economic Organization of the Export Trade of Kashmir and Indian Silks, with Special Reference to their Utilization in the British and French Markets*, London: P.S. King & and Son, Ltd, 1919.
35. Ayjaz Wani, 'Bridging integration: Infrastructure projects in Kashmir', 2023, *ORF*, Available at: https://www.orfonline.org/expert-speak/bridging-integration-infrastructure-projects-in-kashmir
36. Aaratrika Bhaumik, Supreme Court's verdict upholding the abrogation of Article 370 explained, *The Hindu*, 12 December 2023, Available at: https://www.thehindu.com/news/national/supreme-courts-verdict-abrogation-of-article-370-explained/article67626973.ece
37. Shinzani Jain, 'Land Reform and Development in J&K', *NewsClick*, 20 Aug 2019, Available at: https://www.newsclick.in/land-reform-development-jammu-kashmir
38. Ayjaz Wani, 'Bridging integration: Infrastructure projects in Kashmir', *ORF*, 27 Mar 2023, Available at: https://www.orfonline.org/expert-speak/bridging-integration-infrastructure-projects-in-kashmir
39. Mohamed Aslam, 'Land Reforms in Jammu and Kashmir,' *Social Scientist*, Vol. 6, No. 4, 1977, pp. 59-64. https://doi.org/10.2307/3516587
40. T. N. Srinivasan, 'Neoclassical Political Economy, the State and Economic Development T. N. Srinivasan', *Asian Development Review*, Vol 3, 1985, pp. 38-58

41 Anirudh Kumar Prasad, 'Sheikh Abdullah and Land Reforms in Jammu and Kashmir', *Economic and Political Weekly*, Vol. 49, No. 31, 2014, pp. 130-137.
42 Ayjaz Wani, 'Kashmir's Transformation from Terrorism To Tourism', ORF, 2023, Available at: https://www.orfonline.org/expert-speak/kashmirs-transformation-from-terrorism-to-tourism
43 ibid.
44 'Report of the CAG of India for the year ended 31 March 1989, Government of Jammu and Kashmir', Comptroller and Auditor General of India, Available at: https://calm.cag.gov.in//storage/media/jtx49agGh9qgsWC9AarVzpE7LJwZ6Eu38pdpKCMY.pdf
45 'Report of the CAG of India for the year 1984-85, Government of Jammu and Kashmir', Comptroller and Auditor General of India, Available at: https://calm.cag.gov.in//storage/media/5VaP7iLB7JbpjJXYID5QF4Rtiey9gS2T7PSbgu5l.pdf
46 'Report of the CAG of India for the year 1979-80, Government of Jammu and Kashmir', Comptroller and Auditor General of India, Available at: https://calm.cag.gov.in//storage/media/VX6KDSXW8TRRi0OC7ubAsf7514lzqs5L1ux2L4gY.pdf
47 'Report of the CAG of India for the year 1984-85, Government of Jammu and Kashmir', Comptroller and Auditor General of India, Available at: https://calm.cag.gov.in//storage/media/jtx49agGh9qgsWC9AarVzpE7LJwZ6Eu38pdpKCMY.pdf
48 Siddhartha Guha Ray (2022), 'Exodus Of Kashmiri Pandits—Claims Versus Reality', *Outlook India*, 06 Apr 2022, Available at URL: https://www.outlookindia.com/art-entertainment/exodus-of-kashmiri-pandits-claims-versus-

reality-news-190344
49. 'Annual Report 1995-96', Ministry of Home Affairs, Government of India, p. 115.
50. 'Annual Report 2004-05', Ministry of Home Affairs, Government of India, p. 32
51. 'Annual Report 1995-96', Ministry of Home Affairs, Government of India, p. 106-07
52. 'Report of the CAG of India for the year ended 31st March 1989 Government Of Jammu and Kashmir', Comptroller and Auditor General of India, p. 3.
53. 'Report of the CAG of India for the year ended 31st March 1990 Government Of Jammu and Kashmir', Comptroller and Auditor General of India, p. x.
54. 'Annual Report 1995-96', Ministry of Home Affairs, Government of India, p. 106.
55. 'Report of the CAG of India for the year ended 31st March 1991Government Of Jammu and Kashmir', Comptroller and Auditor General of India, p. xi.
56. 'State Finances Report 2016 - Jammu and Kashmir', *Comptroller and Auditor General (CAG)*, Available at: https://cag.gov.in/ag/jammu-kashmir/en/audit-report/details/26279
57. TCA Sharad Raghavan (2016), 'J&K gets 10% of Central funds with only 1% of population', *The Hindu*, 24 June 2016, Available at: https://www.thehindu.com/news/national/other-states/JampK-gets-10-of-Central-funds-with-only-1-of-population/article14506264.ece
58. "Ibid.
59. GSDP is defined as the total market value of all final goods and services produced within the state in a given period of time, usually a year. It is also considered the sum of value added at every stage of production (the intermediate stages) of all final goods and services produced within a country in

a given period of time, measured on monetary terms. GSDP is an important indicator to measure the growth of different sectors of economy and socio-economic development. Thus, the GSDP estimates are very important for policy makers, administrators, planners and researchers. (As per definition given by Directorate of Economics and Statistics, Govt of India on its website: https://descg.gov.in/stateincome/)

60 The estimate of net state domestic product (NSDP) at current prices is arrived at by deducting the consumption of fixed capital from the gross state domestic product for each sector.

61 *The Economic Survey 2016*, Government of Jammu and Kashmir, Available at: https://ecostatjk.nic.in/pdf/publications/ecosurvey/2016.pdf

62 'Statement Showing State-Wise Distribution Of Income-Tax, Basic Excise Duties And Additional Excise Duties, India Budget 1999-2000', Government of India, Available at: https://www.indiabudget.gov.in/budget_archive/ub1999-2000/rb/annex4.pdf

63 'Report of the Comptroller and Auditor General of India for the year ended March 1999', *Comptroller and Auditor General (CAG)*, Available at: https://calm.cag.gov.in//storage/media/EWFqEfyNXbHF39z4PfDKXEZyEN2eglwdZ0QpySom.pdf

64 'Audit Report for the year ended 31 March 2000' , *Comptroller and Auditor General (CAG)*, Available at: https://cag.gov.in/uploads/old_reports/state/Jammu_Kashmir/rep_2000/civil_ch1.pdf

65 'Audit Report for the year ended 31 March 2000', *Comptroller and Auditor General (CAG)*, Available at: https://cag.gov.in/uploads/old_reports/state/Jammu_Kashmir/rep_2000/civil_overview.pdf

66 'Report of the C&AG of India for the Year 2004 -2005

Appropriation Report, Government of Jammu Kashmir', *Comptroller and Auditor General (CAG)*, Available at: https://cag.gov.in/uploads/old_reports/state/Jammu_Kashmir/rep_2004/civil_over.pdf

67. 'Audit Report (Civil), Jammu and Kashmir For the Year 2007-08', *Comptroller and Auditor General (CAG),* Available at: https://cag.gov.in/en/old-audit-reports/view/13607

68. 'Report of 2009 - Financial and Performance Audit on State Finance of Government of Jammu Kashmir', *Comptroller and Auditor General (CAG),* Available at: https://cag.gov.in/ag/jammu-kashmir/en/audit-report/details/5216

69. 'Report of 2009 - Financial and Performance Audit on State Finance of Government of Jammu Kashmir', Comptroller and Auditor General (CAG), Available at: https://cag.gov.in/ag/jammu-kashmir/en/audit-report/details/5216

70. 'Report of 2010 - Compliance, Financial and Performance Audit on State Finances of Government of Jammu Kashmir', *Comptroller and Auditor General (CAG),* Available at: https://cag.gov.in/ag/jammu-kashmir/en/audit-report/details/5262

71. 'Report of 2010 - Compliance, Financial and Performance Audit on State Finances of Government of Jammu Kashmir', *Comptroller and Auditor General (CAG),* Available at: https://cag.gov.in/ag/jammu-kashmir/en/audit-report/details/5262

72. 'Corruption Offences (States/UTs)', NCRB, Available at: https://ncrb.gov.in/en/node/2973

73. 'SAC puts question mark on implementation of around Rs 1800 crores worth schemes in J&K', *Daily Excelsior,* 16 April 2018, Available at: https://www.dailyexcelsior.com/sac-puts-question-mark-implementation-around-rs-1800-crores-worth-schemes-jk/

74. 'SAC puts question mark on implementation of around Rs 1800 crores worth schemes in J&K', *Daily Excelsior,* 16 April

2018, Available at: https://www.dailyexcelsior.com/sac-puts-question-mark-implementation-around-rs-1800-crores-worth-schemes-jk/

75 Ritika Jain (2018), 'Jammu and Kashmir is India's most corrupt state, says anti-graft body chairman', *The Print*, 02 August 2018, Available at: https://theprint.in/india/governance/jammu-and-kashmir-is-indias-most-corrupt-state-says-anti-graft-body-chairman/91425/

76 Mir Ehsan (2015), 'J&K's law officers are relatives of politicians, babus and judges', *The Indian Express*, 23 July 2015, Available at: https://indianexpress.com/article/india/india-others/jks-law-officers-are-relatives-of-politicians-babus-and-judges/

77 'BCCI to probe alleged Jammu & Kashmir Cricket Association scam', *NTDV*, 31 March 2012, Available at: https://sports.ndtv.com/cricket/bcci-to-probe-alleged-jammu--kashmir-cricket-association-scam-1556754

78 'Farooq Abdullah Charged by CBI in Scam Linked To J&K Cricket Body', *NDTV*, 16 July 2018, Available at: https://www.ndtv.com/india-news/ex-jammu-and-kashmir-chief-minister-farooq-abdullah-charged-by-cbi-in-scam-linked-to-state-cricket-b-1884181

79 'Farooq Abdullah named in ED chargesheet on alleged J&K cricket association scam', *Scroll*, 26 July 2022, Available at: https://scroll.in/latest/1029124/farooq-abdullah-named-in-ed-chargesheet-on-alleged-j-k-cricket-association-scam

80 'Chargesheet Filed Against Farooq Abdullah In Money Laundering Case', *NDTV*, 26 July 2022, Available at: https://www.ndtv.com/india-news/chargesheet-filed-against-farooq-abdullah-in-money-laundering-case-3194788

81 'Frankly Speaking With Satya Pal Malik | Full Interview', *Times Now*, 27 October 2018, Available at: https://www.

timesnownews.com/videos/news/india/frankly-speaking-with-satya-pal-malik-full-interview/13590

82 Mudasir Ahmad, 'J&K Bank Comes Under Scanner Amid Allegations of Recruitment Scam', *The Wire*, 30 October 2018, Available at: https://thewire.in/politics/jk-bank-comes-under-scanner-amid-allegations-of-recruitment-scam

83 ''Ibid.

84 ''Ibid.

85 '1,100 crore loan scam in J&K Bank; 31 accused chargesheeted', *Deccan Chronicle*, 30 June 2021, Available at: https://www.deccanchronicle.com/nation/current-affairs/290621/1100-crore-loan-scam-in-jk-bank-31-accused-chargesheeted.html

86 ''Ibid.

87 'CBI conducts raids in multi-crore J&K Bank fraud case', *Hindustan Times*, 11 May 2022, Available at: https://www.hindustantimes.com/cities/chandigarh-news/cbi-conducts-raids-in-multi-crore-j-k-bank-fraud-case-101652210795775.html

88 Dinesh Manhotra (2022), 'CBI raids eight locations in multi-crore J&K Bank building scam; incriminating evidence recovered', *IB Times*, 10 May 2022, Available at: https://www.ibtimes.co.in/cbi-raids-eight-locations-multi-crore-jk-bank-building-scam-incriminating-evidence-recovered-848330

89 'Bank fraud case: ED raids former J&K minister's son Hilal Rather', *Economic Times*, 6 August 2020, Available at: https://economictimes.indiatimes.com/news/politics-and-nation/bank-fraud-case-ed-raids-former-jk-ministers-son-hilal-rather/articleshow/77389870.cms

90 Murali Krishnan (2020), 'Roshni Land Scam and Jammu & Kashmir High Court judgment explained', *Bar & Bench*, 10 December 2020, Available at: https://www.barandbench.

com/columns/litigation-columns/roshni-land-scam-jammu-kashmir-high-court-judgment

91 'J&K administration scraps Roshni Act, says government will retrieve land in six months', *Scroll*, 01 November 2020, Available at: https://scroll.in/latest/977398/j-k-administration-declares-roshni-act-null-and-void-says-will-retrieve-land-in-six-months

92 Murali Krishnan (2020), 'Roshni Land Scam and Jammu & Kashmir High Court judgment explained', *Bar & Bench*, 10 December 2020, Available at: https://www.barandbench.com/columns/litigation-columns/roshni-land-scam-jammu-kashmir-high-court-judgment

93 'Parliament approves Resolution to repeal Article 370; paves way to truly integrate J&K with Indian Union,' *Press Information Bureau*, 6 August 2019, Available at: https://pib.gov.in/newsite/PrintRelease.aspx?relid=192505

94 ibid.

95 Pramod Kumar, 'SC upholds constitutional validity of abrogation of Article 370, bifurcation of Jammu and Kashmir,' *The Statesman,* 11 December 2013, Available at: https://www.thestatesman.com/india/supreme-court-upholds-centres-decision-to-abrogate-article-370-1503248801.html

96 Billy Perrigo, 'The Indian Government Is Revoking Kashmir's Special Status. Here's What That Means,' *Time*, 5 August 2019, Available at: https://time.com/5644356/india-kashmir-article-370/

97 'Annual Reports,' Ministry of Home Affairs, Government of India, Available at: https://www.mha.gov.in/en/documents/annual-reports read till here.

98 Zulfikar Majid, 'Terror funding case: NIA raids continue across J&K,' *The Deccan Herald*, 5 December 2023, Available at: https://www.deccanherald.com/india/jammu-and-kashmir/

anti-terror-case-nia-searches-in-5-jk-districts-2797253

99 Naveed Iqbal, 'Newsmaker | From democracy icon to terror accused, Waheed Para fell out with Centre,' *The Indian Express*, 27 May 2022, https://indianexpress.com/article/political-pulse/how-pdp-waheed-para-with-centre-7939822/

100 'Terror-funding case: NIA arrests former J&K MLA Rashid Engineer,' 10 August 2019, Available at: https://www.thehindu.com/news/national/funding-case-nia-arrests-former-jk-mla-rashid-engineer/article28970722

101 'MHA says 40 per cent decline in militant recruitments this year,' *The Today*, 13 July 2019, Available at: https://www.facebook.com/TodayIn/posts/2463615893694975/?paipv=0&eav=AfbiYqzn1aqXMXr5bjxyvQTfgnhgkQWmq2uXhczIG5NcxA2zBM0_oTczeQ3cRDReE&_rdr

102 'Abrogation of Article 370 ensures Women of Jammu and Kashmir as citizens,' *The Only Kashmir,* 29 July 2023, Available at: https://www.o in/24660/abrogation-of-article-370-ensures-women-of-jammu-and-ka equal-citizens/

103 Nestula Hebbar & Vijaita Singh, 'Government jobs to be reserved for of J&K, says Centre,', *The Hindu,* 1 April 2020, Available at: https://w thehindu.com/news/national/govt-jobs-to-be-reserved-only-for-domic says-centre/article31224164.ece

104 '4 years of Article 370 repeal | 92 per cent decrease in stone pelting, 9 cent in hartal calls', *Greater Kashmir,* 4 August 2023, Available at: http greaterkashmir.com/kashmir/4-years-of-article-370-repeal-92-decrease pelting-90-in-hartal-calls-2/

105 Deeptiman Tiwary, 'MHA data: 88 per cent dip in J&K stone-pelting to 2019,' *The Indian Express,* 4 August 2021, Available at: https://indi com/article/india/mha-data-88-per-cent-dip-in-jk-stone-pelting-comp to-2019-7437047/

106 Naveed Iqbal, 'Active militants in J&K brought down to double digit *The Indian Express,* 31 December 2022, Available at: https://indianexp com/article/cities/srinagar/active-militants-jammu-kashmir-jk-brough police-8353900/

107 '4 years of Article 370 abrogation: Has security situation improved in J&K?', *First Post*, 05 August 2023, Available at: https://www.firstpost.com/explainers/article-370-abrogation-has-security-situation-improved-in-jammu-and-kashmir-12961842.html

108 Neha Aggarwal (2023), 'Analyzing the transition of Panchayati Raj Institutions in Jammu and Kashmir', *J&K Policy Institute*, 8 July 2023, https://www.jkpi.org/analyzing-the-transition-of-panchayati-raj-institutions-in-jammu-and-kashmir/

109 Ananya Bhardwaj (2019), 'Modi govt has sent Rs 800 crores to J&K panchayats but no projects planned yet to spend it', *The Print*, 11 September 2019, Available at: https://theprint.in/india/modi-govt-has-sent-rs-800-crores-to-jk-panchayats-but-no-projects-planned-yet-to-spend-it/286945/

110 'Centre unveils Rs 1,08,621 crore budget of J&K for 2021-22', *The Dispatch*, 17 March 2021, Available at: https://www.thedispatch.in/centre-unveils-rs-108-621-crore-budget-of-jk-for-2021-22/

111 'Budget (2020-2021), Jammu and Kashmir', Government of India, Available at: https://jakfinance.nic.in/budget/budget2021/Budget per cent20Speech per cent202020-21.pdf

112 'Budget (2021-2022), Jammu and Kashmir', Government of India, Available at: https://jakfinance.nic.in/budget/budget2122/2 per cent20Budget per cent20at per cent20a per cent20Glance per cent20(English) per cent202021-22.pdf

113 'Report No. 2 of the year 2022 - Audit Report of the Comptroller and Auditor General of India on the Union Territory Finances for the year ended 31 March 2021, Government of Union Territory of Jammu and Kashmir', Comptroller and Auditor General (CAG), Available at: https://cag.gov.in/ag/jammu-kashmir/en/audit-report/

details/116681
114 'Central Sector Scheme for Industrial Development of Jammu and Kashmir', Government of India, Available: https://dpiit.gov.in/notification-new-central-sector-scheme-industrial-development-jammu-and-kashmir
115 'Report No.1 of the year 2023 - Union Territory Finances Audit Report for the year ended 31 March 2022, Government of Union Territory of Jammu and Kashmir', Comptroller and Auditor General (CAG), Available at: https://cag.gov.in/ag/jammu-kashmir/en/audit-report/details/118551
116 'Supplementary Demands for Grants of the Union Territory of Jammu & Kashmir (With Legislature) for 2021-2022 and Budget for 2022-2023', Government of India, Available at: https://jakfinance.nic.in/budget/budget2223/1 per cent20Budget per cent20Speech per cent202022-23.pdf
117 ibid.
118 'Supplementary Demands for Grants of the Union Territory of Jammu & Kashmir (With Legislature) for 2022-2023 and Budget for 2023-2024', Budget at a Glance, Government of India, Available at: https://jakfinance.nic.in/budget/budget2324/Budget per cent20at per cent20a per cent20Glance per cent202023-24 per cent20(English).pdf
119 ibid.
120 'Jammu and Kashmir Industrial Policy 2021', Government of Jammu and Kashmir, Available at: https://investjammu.in/wp-content/uploads/2021/04/Jammu-and-Kashmir-Industrial-Policy-2021-30.pdf
121 ibid.
122 'J&K Eyes Rs 23000 Crores Investment, Inks 456 MoUs', *Kashmir Observer*, 6 April 2021, Available at: https://kashmirobserver.net/2021/04/06/jk-eyes-rs-23000-crores-investment-inks-456-mous/

123 'New Central Sector Scheme for Industrial Development of Union Territory of Jammu & Kashmir', *The Gazette of India*, 19 February 2021, Available at: https://jknis.dpiit.gov.in/Document/Notification-J&K-NewPolicy-23February2021.pdf

124 'Two years since Article 370 abrogation: What has changed in Jammu & Kashmir?', 5 August 2021, *The Times of India*, Available at: https://timesofindia.indiatimes.com/india/two-years-since-article-370-abrogation-what-has-changed-in-jammu-kashmir/articleshow/85057707.cms

125 'Jammu and Kashmir Industrial Land Allotment Policy 2021-30', Government of Jammu and Kashmir, Available at: https://industrieskashmir.nic.in/industrieskashmir/landallotmentpolicy2021.pdf

126 'J&K approves new land allotment policy for entrepreneurs', *The Indian Express*, 23 January 2021, Available at: https://indianexpress.com/article/india/jk-approves-new-land-allotment-policy-for-entrepreneurs-7157990/

127 ibid.

128 'JK inks 456 MOUs for potential investment', *Kashmir Vision*, 7 April 2021, Available at: https://kashmirvision.in/2021/04/07/jk-inks-456-mous-for-potential-investment/

129 Zulfikar Majid (2021), 'J&K government signs MoUs worth Rs 18,300 crore with country's real estate investors', *Deccan Herald*, 27 December 2021, Available at: https://www.deccanherald.com/india/jk-government-signs-mous-worth-rs-18300-crore-with-countrys-real-estate-investors-1065315.html

130 'J&K got Rs 1,547 crores investment in 2022-23, says MoS Home Nityanand Rai', *The Business Standard*, 14 March 2023, Available at: https://www.business-standard.com/article/economy-policy/j-k-got-rs-1-547-crores-investment-in-2022-23-says-mos-home-nityanand-rai-123031400887_1.html

131 Peerzada Ashiq (2023), 'UAE's Emaar becomes first overseas company to start a mega-mall project in Kashmir', *The Hindu,* 19 March 2023, Available at: https://www.thehindu.com/news/national/other-states/uaes-emaar-becomes-first-overseas-company-to-start-a-mega-mall-project-in-kashmir/article66638253.ece

132 'J-K: New Industrial Policy draws Rs 2200 crores investment in 1 year, generates 10,000 jobs', *ANI News,* 10 June 2023, Available at: https://www.aninews.in/news/national/general-news/j-k-new-industrial-policy-draws-rs-2200-crores-investment-in-1-year-generates-10000-jobs20230610134826/

133 'J&K goes all out to woo real estate investments,' *The Times of India,* 29 December 2021, Available at: http://timesofindia.indiatimes.com/articleshow/88573936.cms?utm_source=contentofinterest&utm_medium=text&utm_campaign=cppst

134 Shaib Mohammad Shaib (2019), 'Tourism Industry Of Jammu & Kashmir: Challenges and Opportunities', *International Journal of Research and Analytical Reviews,* 06 (1): 303-308, Available at: https://ijrar.org/papers/IJRAR19J1511.pdf

135 'Jammu and Kashmir: Tourism triumphs in 2023', *The Economic Times,* 2 January 2024, Available at: https://travel.economictimes.indiatimes.com/blog/jammu-and-kashmir-tourism-triumphs-in-2023/106476301

136 'Jammu and Kashmir Tourism Policy-2020', Government of Jammu and Kashmir, Available at: http://jammutourism.gov.in/pdf/TP2020.pdf

137 'Over 75 J&K villages being brought under 'Tourist Village Network' programme: officials', *Greater Kashmir,* 07 Feb 2022, Available at: https://www.greaterkashmir.com/business/over-75-jk-villages-being-brought-under-tourist-village-

network-programme-officials
138 'J&K govt, OYO launch 'Crown of Incredible India' home-stay initiative', *Live Mint*, 10 February 2022, Available at: https://www.livemint.com/news/india/jk-govt-oyo-launch-crown-of-incredible-india-home-stay-initiative-11644507879524.html
139 Ashiq Hussain, 'G20 working group meeting concludes in Srinagar,' *The Hindustan Times*, 24 May 2023, Available at: https://www.hindustantimes.com/india-news/g20-delegates-go-sightseeing-in-srinagar-amid-rain-experience-kashmir-s-tourism-potential-and-hospitality-try-traditional-attire-and-yoga-101684927475971.html
140 'Jammu and Kashmir Film Policy-2021', Government of Jammu and Kashmir, Available at: https://jkgad.nic.in/common/showOrder.aspx?actCode=O38884
141 ibid.
142 ibid.
143 'Film era of 80's returning to J&K, over 300 movies shot so far in UT: LG', *Kashmir Dispatch*, 18 August 2023, Available at: https://kashmirdespatch.com/film-era-of-80s-returning-to-jk-over-300-movies-shot-so-far-in-ut-lg/
144 'Jammu and Kashmir IT/ITES-2020', Government of Kashmir, Available at: https://www.jkit.nic.in/policies/jkItEsPolicy2020.pdf
145 ibid.
146 ibid.
147 ibid.
148 ibid.
149 'IT-hub to come up in Srinagar outskirts', *Daily Excelsior*, 11 March 2021, Available at: https://www.dailyexcelsior.com/it-hub-to-come-up-in-srinagar-outskirts/
150 'Jammu and Kashmir IT/ITES-2020', Government of

Kashmir, Available at: https://www.jkit.nic.in/policies/jkItEsPolicy2020.pdf

151 Mukeet Akmali (2021), '2 million square feet IT hub to come up in J&K', *Greater Kashmir*, 06 Sep 2021, Available at: https://www.greaterkashmir.com/todays-paper/front-page/2-million-square-feet-it-hub-to-come-up-in-jk

152 'Jammu and Kashmir Wool Processing, Handloom, Handicrafts Policy -2020', Government of Jammu and Kashmir, Available at: https://jkindustriescommerce.nic.in/Orders%202020/54%20IND%20of%202020.pdf

153 ibid.

Select Bibliography

Aslam, Mohamed (1977) 'Land Reforms in Jammu and Kashmir', *Social Scientist*, Vol. 6, No. 4, pp. 59-64.

Bamzai, P N K (1988) *Socio-Economic History of Kashmir (1846-1925)*. New Delhi: Metropolitan.

Behera, Navnita C. (2000) *State, Identity and Violence: Jammu, Kashmir and Ladakh*. New Delhi: Manohar.

Ernst, Waltraud and Biswamoy Pati, eds. (2007) *India's Princely States: People, Princes and Colonialism*. London: Routledge

Ganguly, Sumit (1996) 'Explaining the Kashmir Insurgency: Political Mobilization and Institutional Decay', *International Security*, Vol. 21, No. 2, pp. 76-107.

Gani, A. (1990) 'Industrial Relations in Jammu and Kashmir', *Indian Journal of Agrarian Relations*, Vol. 26, Issue 1, pp. 53-67.

Habib, Irfan (1999) *The Agrarian System of Mughal India, 1556-1707*. New Delhi: Oxford University Press.

Hangloo, R. L. (2000) *The State in Medieval Kashmir*. New Delhi: Manohar.

Jehangir, Sheikh Khalid (2022) *The Two Kashmirs: A Comparative Analysis*. New Delhi: Vitasta.

Kak, Shakti (2007) 'The agrarian system of the princely state of Jammu and Kashmir: A study of colonial settlement policies, 1860-1905', in Ernst, Waltraud and Biswamoy Pati, eds. (2007) *India's Princely States: People, Princes and Colonialism*. London: Routledge

Khan, M.S. (2002) *The History of Jammu and Kashmir: 1885-1925*, Kashmir: Gulshan.

Lamb, Alaistair (1991) *Kashmir: A Disputed Legacy, 1846-1990*. Hertingfordbury: Oxford Books.

Lawrence, W. R. (1895) *The Valley of Kashmir*. London: Henry Frowde.

Mehdi, Syed Eesar (2020) 'Serving the Militant's Cause: The Role of Indo-Pak State Policies in Sustaining Militancy in Kashmir', *Journal of Asian Security and International Affairs*, Vol. 7, No. 2.

Noorani, A G (2013) *The Kashmir Dispute 1947-2012*. New Delhi: Tulika Books.

Prasad, Anirudh Kumar (2014) 'Sheikh Abdullah and Land Reforms in Jammu and Kashmir', *Economic and Political Weekly*, Vol. 49, No. 31, pp. 130-137.

Rai, Mridu (2004) *Hindu Rulers, Muslim Subjects: Islam, Rights and the History of Kashmir*. Delhi: Permanent Black.

Rawlley, Ratan Chand (1919) *The Silk Industry and Trade: A Study in the Economic Organization of the Export Trade of Kashmir and Indian Silks, with Special Reference to their Utilization in the British and French Markets*. London: P.S. King & Son.

Schofield, Victoria (1996) *Kashmir in the Crossfire*. London: I.B. Taurus Publishers.

Shaib, Mohammad (2019) 'Tourism Industry Of Jammu & Kashmir: Challenges and Opportunities', *International Journal of Research and Analytical Reviews*, Vol. 6, No. 1, pp. 303-308.

Teng, M K, R K K Bhat and S Kaul (1977) *Kashmir: Constitutional History and Documents*. New Delhi: Light and Life Publishers.

Thorp, Robert (1868) *Cashmere Misgovernment*, Calcutta: R.M. Lewis.

Varshney, Ashutosh (1991) 'India, Pakistan, and Kashmir: Antinomies of Nationalism', *Asian Survey*, Vol. 31, No. 11, pp. 997-1019.

Younghusband, Francis (1911) *Kashmir*. London: Adam and Charles Black.

Zutshi, Chitralekha (2003) *Languages of Belonging – Islam, Regional Identity and the Making of Kashmir*. Delhi: Permanent Black.

Reports

'Accounts at a Glance 2020-21', *Government of Union Territory of Jammu and Kashmir,* Available at: https://cag.gov.in/uploads/state_accounts_report/account-report-J-K-Accounts-at-a-glance-2021-22-English-09-01-2023-063bd0694c36ed5-89604395.pdf

'Accounts at a Glance 2021-22', *Government of Union Territory of Jammu and Kashmir,* Available at: https://cag.gov.in/uploads/state_accounts_report/account-report-J-K-Accounts-at-a-glance-2021-22-English-09-01-2023-063bd0694c36ed5-89604395.pdf

'Accounts at a Glance 2010-11', *Government of Jammu and Kashmir,* Available at: https://cag.gov.in/uploads/state_accounts_report/JK_Account_Glance_2010_11.pdf

'Accounts at a Glance 2011-12', *Government of Jammu and Kashmir,* Available at: https://cag.gov.in/uploads/state_accounts_report/JK_Account_Glance_2011_12.pdf

'Accounts at a Glance 2012-13', *Government of Jammu and Kashmir,* Available at: https://cag.gov.in/uploads/state_accounts_report/JK_Account_Glance_2012_13.pdf

'Accounts at a Glance 2013-14', *Government of Jammu and Kashmir,* Available at: https://cag.gov.in/uploads/state_accounts_report/JK_Accout_Glance_2013_14.pdf

'Accounts at a Glance 2014-15', *Government of Jammu and*

Kashmir, Available at: https://cag.gov.in/uploads/state_accounts_report/JK_April_2014_15.pdf

'Accounts at a Glance 2015-16', *Government of Jammu and Kashmir,* Available at: https://cag.gov.in/uploads/state_accounts_report/JK_April_2015_16.pdf

'Accounts at a Glance 2016-17', *Government of Jammu and Kashmir,* Available at: https://cag.gov.in/uploads/state_accounts_report/JK_Account_Glance_2016_17.pdf

'Accounts at a Glance 2017-18', *Government of Jammu and Kashmir,* Available at: https://cag.gov.in/uploads/state_accounts_report/account-report-J-K-Accounts-at-a-glance-2017-18-05f9133170bd1c8-21016002.pdf

'Annual Report 1995-96', *Ministry of Home Affairs, Government of India,* Available at: https://www.mha.gov.in/sites/default/files/REPORT_1995_96_12022021.pdf

'Annual Report 2004-05', *Ministry of Home Affairs, Government of India,* Available at: https://www.mha.gov.in/sites/default/files/AnnualReport_04_05.pdf

'Annual Report 2021-22', *Ministry of Home Affairs, Government of India,* Available at: https://www.mha.gov.in/sites/default/files/AnnualReport202122_24112022%5B1%5D.pdf

'Audit Report for the year ended 31 March 2000', *Comptroller and Auditor General of India,* Available at: https://cag.gov.in/en/old-audit-reports/view/14486

'Audit Report, Jammu and Kashmir For the Year 1999-2000', *Comptroller and Auditor General of India,* Available at: https://cag.gov.in/en/old-audit-reports/view/14486.pdf

'Audit Report, (Civil) Jammu and Kashmir for the Year 2000-01', *Comptroller and Auditor General of India,* Available at: https://cag.gov.in/en/old-audit-reports/view/14408

'Audit Report for the year ended 31 March 2004 Government of Jammu and Kashmir', *Comptroller and Auditor General of India,* Available at: https://cag.gov.in/en/old-audit-reports/view/14278

'Audit Report for the year ended 31 March 2008 Government of Jammu and Kashmir', *Comptroller and Auditor General of India*, Available at: https://cag.gov.in/en/old-audit-reports/view/13607

'Audit Report (Civil), Jammu and Kashmir for the Year 2007-08', *Comptroller and Auditor General of India*, Available at: https://cag.gov.in/en/old-audit-reports/view/13607

'Budget (2013-2014)', *Government of Jammu and Kashmir*, Available at: https://www.jakfinance.nic.in/budget06.html

'Budget (2014-2015)', *Government of Jammu and Kashmir*, Available at: https://www.jakfinance.nic.in/budget05.html

'Budget (2015-2016)', *Government of Jammu and Kashmir*, Available at: https://www.jakfinance.nic.in/budget04.html

'Budget (2016-2017)', *Government of Jammu and Kashmir*, Available at: https://www.jakfinance.nic.in/budget03.html

'Budget (2017-2018)', *Government of Jammu and Kashmir*, Available at: https://www.jakfinance.nic.in/budget02.html

'Budget (2018-2019)', *Government of Jammu and Kashmir*, Available at: https://www.jakfinance.nic.in/budget01.html

'Budget (2019-2020)', *Government of Union Territory of Jammu and Kashmir*, Available at: https://www.jakfinance.nic.in/budget3.html

'Budget (2020-2021)', *Government of Union Territory of Jammu and Kashmir*, Available at: https://www.jakfinance.nic.in/budget1.html

'Budget (2021-2022)', *Government of Union Territory of Jammu and Kashmir*, Available at: https://www.jakfinance.nic.in/budgetnew.html

'Budget (2022-2023)', *Government of Union Territory of Jammu and Kashmir*, Available at: https://www.jakfinance.nic.in/budget2022-23.html

'Budget (2023-2024)', *Government of Union Territory of Jammu and Kashmir*, Available at: https://www.jakfinance.nic.in/

budget2023-24.html

'Corruption Offences (States/UTs)', *National Crime Records Bureau (NCRB)*, Available at: https://ncrb.gov.in/en/node/2973

'Economic Survey 2017', *Government of Jammu and Kashmir*, Available at: https://jakfinance.nic.in/SROs/SRO_2017/EconomicSurvey2017.pdf

'Report of the Comptroller and Auditor General of India for the year 1978-79 Government Of Jammu and Kashmir', *Comptroller and Auditor General of India*, Available at: https://calm.cag.gov.in//storage/media/VX6KDSXW8TRRi0OC7ubAsf7514lzqs5L1ux2L4gY.pdf

'Report of the Comptroller and Auditor General of India for the year 1979-80 Government Of Jammu and Kashmir', *Comptroller and Auditor General of India*, Available at: https://calm.cag.gov.in//storage/media/VX6KDSXW8TRRi0OC7ubAsf7514lzqs5L1ux2L4gY.pdf

'Report of the Comptroller and Auditor General of India for the year 1984-85 Government Of Jammu and Kashmir', *Comptroller and Auditor General of India (CAG)*, Available at: https://calm.cag.gov.in//storage/media/5VaP7iLB7JbpjJXYID5QF4Rtiey9gS2T7PSbgu5l.pdf

'Report of the Comptroller and Auditor General of India for the year ended 31st March 1989 Government Of Jammu and Kashmir', *Comptroller and Auditor General of India*, Available at: https://calm.cag.gov.in//storage/media/jtx49agGh9qgsWC9AarVzpE7LJwZ6Eu38pdpKCMY.pdf

'Report of the Comptroller and Auditor General of India for the year ended 31st March 1990 Government of Jammu and Kashmir', *Comptroller and Auditor General of India*, Available at: https://calm.cag.gov.in//storage/media/r80trHIimc4LhqtPHXwWLfyr6aPVxGZkcjVwPxdg.pdf

'Report of the Comptroller and Auditor General of India for the year ended 31st March 1991 Government Of Jammu and Kashmir', *Comptroller and Auditor General of India*, Available at: https://calm.cag.gov.in//storage/media/43d848dmy0DA8hIN77DuIHZ1Ke0uiiFoOlcQYTpJ.pdf

'Report of the Comptroller and Auditor General of India for the year ended March 1999', *Comptroller and Auditor General (CAG)*, Available at: https://calm.cag.gov.in//storage/media/EWFqEfyNXbHF39z4PfDKXEZyEN2eglwdZ0QpySom.pdf

'Report of the C&AG of India for the Year 2004 -2005 Appropriation Report, Government of Jammu Kashmir', *Comptroller and Auditor General (CAG)*, Available at: https://cag.gov.in/uploads/old_reports/state/Jammu_Kashmir/rep_2004/civil_over.pdf

'Report of 2009 - Financial and Performance Audit on State Finance of Government of Jammu Kashmir', *Comptroller and Auditor General (CAG)*, Available at: https://cag.gov.in/ag/jammu-kashmir/en/audit-report/details/5216

'Report of 2010 - Compliance, Financial and Performance Audit on State Finances of Government of Jammu Kashmir', *Comptroller and Auditor General (CAG)*, Available at: https://cag.gov.in/ag/jammu-kashmir/en/audit-report/details/5262

'Report of the C&AG of India for the year ended 31 March 1999, Government of Jammu and Kashmir', *Comptroller and Auditor General (CAG)*, Available at: https://calm.cag.gov.in/ebooks/report-of-the-c-ag-of-india-for-the-year-ended-31-march-1999-government-of-jammu-and-kashmir

'Report of 2010 - Compliance, Financial and Performance Audit on State Finances of Government of Jammu Kashmir', *Comptroller and Auditor General (CAG)*, Available at: https://cag.gov.in/en/audit-report/details/5262

'Report No. 2 of 2020 - State Finances, Government of Jammu & Kashmir', *Comptroller and Auditor General (CAG)*, Available at: https://cag.gov.in/en/audit-report/details/113556

'State Finances Report 2016 - Jammu and Kashmir', *Comptroller and Auditor General (CAG)*, Available at: https://cag.gov.in/ag/jammu-kashmir/en/audit-report/details/26279

'Statement Showing State-Wise Distribution of Income-Tax, Basic Excise Duties and Additional Excise Duties, India Budget 1999-2000', *Government of India*, Available at: https://www.indiabudget.gov.in/budget_archive/ub1999-2000/rb/annex4.pdf

'The Economic Survey 2016', *Government of Jammu and Kashmir*, Available at: https://ecostatjk.nic.in/pdf/publications/ecosurvey/2016.pdf